Turin

Footprint

Ben Donald

Contents

Listings

About the author

Ben Donald is a freelance travel writer whose journalism has appeared in the (London) *Times* and various travel magazines such as *Traveller*, *Global Adventure* and *Travel Africa*. He is also responsible for the distribution of BBC programmes into Italy. He is a keen independent traveller, fluent in a number of languages including Italian, and has lived and worked in several countries, including a year teaching English to teenagers in Turin. Ben is the author of *Footprint Bologna* and also *The Book of Cities*, published by Pavilion Books in Spring 2004.

Acknowledgements

There are people and forces from past and present who have helped me write this guide. Huge thanks are due to Paola Musolino and her colleagues at the Turin tourist bureau for reading through and correcting the text, and for supplying much useful additional information. I am also indebted to their London colleague, Gaby Marcon, for her insights, nuances and general input. My wife, Merida, was wonderful in unfailingly providing delicious food for thought and inspiration, and for putting up with my absence as I slaved away at words into the night. But this book is really dedicated to Max and Marco, who I had the fortune to bump into one summer night in piazza Albarello 11 years ago, and who subsequently taught me all the Italian slang I know, became the face of Turin and, best of all, eternal friends. It is a great honour to have the chance to write a guide to your weird and wonderful city, a unique world where stuff just happens and which disappears when you leave... E' sempre li dove sai tu!

Introducing Turin

Baroque castles and royal palaces, regal arcaded squares and stately tree-lined boulevards, all crowned by a breathtaking alpine backdrop. Turin displays all the grace of the Savoy family, a name that has become synonymous with the refined and luxurious. It was a style that bred a sophisticated salon society of intellectuals and thinkers; in the city's rarefied aristocratic and artistic cafés the idea of an Italian Republic was converted from a twinkle into a reality. Yet beneath Turin's classic exterior lurks the rebellious and possessed soul of an awkward child prodigy, with a personality that shys away from the normal Italian froth and bubble. It is the product of an incongruous collection of assets and eccentric character traits that combine to cast a peculiar sense of alchemy, like a shroud, over the city. It is these attractions, veiled in alpine mist and mystery, and for so long obscured by the fog of ignorance and stereotypes, that have kept Turin one of Italy's best-kept secrets.

Italian eccentricity

Behind the majestic façades, Piedmont's capital is home to an oddball collection of treasures. Not least of these are the infamous Turin Shroud and the unexpected Egyptian Museum, the largest of its type outside Cairo. Combined with the city's mythical winter fog and a number of myths and legends, this has granted Turin status as a centre of black magic. Turin is also the city of the black and white stripes of Juventus football club, a vibrant contemporary arts and music scene and the birthplace of Italian cinema. It is food and drink heaven – even for Italy – as the home of Lavazza coffee, Martini and the best Italian chocolate. And yes, it is the engine of Italy and the city that Fiat built, a city that produced the Cinquecento and other retro favourites still as popular as the Mini Coopers that once roared through the city in the famous car chase of *The Italian Job*.

Alpine air

Turin stands as a gateway to the Alps, on the cusp of the great rice plain to the east. In one direction stand the vineyards of Barolo, the king of Italian wines, and the magic climate that produces the prized white truffle; in the other, the winter and summer playground of the valley of Aosta culminating in two of the Alps' most spectacular peaks, the Matterhorn and Mont Blanc. Not before time these assets have put Turin on the map both for jaded and prejudiced Italians and tourists who previously only had eyes for the cities of the Victorian Grand Tour: Venice, Florence, Rome and Naples. The advent of the Winter Olympics in 2006 brings a focus to this renewed interest, although in reality, to those in the know, a movement was already fermenting. For so long exiled just like the Royal family to which the city was home for four centuries, Turin is again being crowned as one of Italy's most treasured, innovative and dynamic cities.

At a glance

Turin is a long oblong of a city with north-south boulevards traversed by a grid of side streets. With a few exceptions, most of the city's sights, retail and nightlife lie within the boundary of Corso Regina Margherita to the north and Corso Vittorio Emanuele II to the south, piazza Statuto to the West and the river Po to the east.

Centre – Royal Turin

In a city symmetrically balanced by many fine squares, piazza Castello is Turin's most majestic, a visual recorder of the city's history and a logical starting point for any visitor. Cloistered by a quadrangle of porticoes, three sides of the piazza are flanked by the baroque and neoclassical façades of the former residences of the House of Savoy and Turin's main theatre. Set back in the northern side is the Savoy's Royal Palace and Gardens. Turin's cathedral is annexed to the Palazzo Reale with Filippo Juvarra's famous scissor staircase inside. At the centre of the piazza stands the palazzo Madama, a former Savoy castle built on the original eastern Roman city gate.

Northeast – University and Borgo Po

Between the atmospheric arches of via Po and Corso Regina Margherita is the heart of Turin's university life, a tight network of lively and youthfully shabby streets. At the end of via Po the street opens out into piazza Vittorio Veneto. It slopes down to the banks of the Po and the Murazzi, scene of riverside café life by day and Turin's most subversive nocturnal life by night. Rising above this quarter is the Mole Antonelliana, Turin's equivalent of the Eiffel Tower, with the Museo Nazionale del Cinema inside, the best cinema museum in Europe. On the right bank, in sharp contrast, a verdant screen of undulating hills rises up. At the foot of them stands the neoclassical church of the Gran Madre; further up, the church of Santa Maria in Monte and above that the former royal Villa della Regina. In the distance like a guardian angel stands the basilica of the Superga. By night and especially in winter, the brooding atmosphere of this scene inspires belief that Turin is a centre of occult activity.

Southeast
Many of Turin's most notable and world-famous museums are housed within this quarter, around the narrow streets south of via Po. The Museo Egizio contains the largest collection of Egyptian art and artefacts outside Cairo while the Galleria Sabauda is home to the city's collection of old master paintings. Further south, across Corso Vittorio Emanuele II and east of the main station, is the Parco Valentino, containing a botanical garden, a majestic baroque palace and a faux-medieval castle. Fiat (Fabbrica Italiana Automobili Torino), the city's most famous company, is based here in the city's southern suburbs. Production continues at the Mirafiori plant but the former Lingotto factory, with its famous roof-top testing track, has been converted into a supermodern museum-cum -conference centre.

Southwest
Turin's Champs-Elysees, the via Roma, links piazza Castello with piazza San Carlo Felice and the main station, Porta Nuova. Via Roma is a catwalk of promenading torinesi, home to the city's flashiest boutiques. At its midpoint is piazza San Carlo, a square still redolent of the city's famous literary café life. West of via Roma, Turin is at its most Parisian with the area of art nouveau architecture appropriately found on Corso Francia. On via Cernaia are the remnants of Turin's former citadel, all but destroyed by Franco-Spanish invaders, and the underground passages that were the scene of a heroic defense of the city. Beyond that isTurin's older football stadium, the Stadio Comunale, training ground of Juventus and soon-to-be Olympic theatre and HQ of Torino FC.

Northwest – Roman Turin

The alleyways north of via Garibaldi have recently come alive with bars and are the favoured venue come aperitif time – a tradition that has belatedly come home to hard-working Turin. These are the streets of the original Roman settlement. Here, the weekly market is an almost North African bazaar of colour, smells and bargains. North of piazza Repubblica is the site of Turin's monthly flea market, *il Gran Balon*. Further north around the freight station are post-industrial warehouses that have become some of Turin's most original clubs and late lounges. On the far northern outskirts is the Stadio delle Alpi, the main football stadium and to the west the piazza Statuto and the station of Porta Susa, soon to be transformed into Turin's Eurostar link in time for the 2006 Winter Olympics.

Castles and country retreats

At all points of the compass Turin is surrounded by castles that were once the converted country retreats of the Savoy dukes. To the southwest is the hunting lodge of Stupinigi; to the south the hilltop fortress of Moncalieri, and beyond the hills, the incongruously majestic palace in Aglié. To the west stand both Rivoli castle with its modern art museum and the royal lodge at Venaria Reale. Further north is the decadent red-brick palace of Racconigi.

Excursions

Turin provides a good base for a huge variety of daytrips. An hour or so to the northwest, beyond the pretty carnival town of Ivrea, lies the Val d'Aosta. From Aosta itself the road leads towards the Alps passing the famous ski resorts of Cervinia – symbolized by the Matterhorn – and Courmayeur. Savoy castles and fortresses line the route due west to valleys of Susa which will be the playground for the 2006 Olympic Games. Beautiful walks are also to be enjoyed in the Gran Paradiso National Park. To the east lie the rich wine-growing villages of Alba and Barolo. Nearby are the towns of Asti and Alessandria and the thermal waters at Acqui Terme.

★ **Best**

Ten of the best

1 **Museo Egizio** The largest collection of Egyptiania outside Cairo: whole mummies, tombs and sarcophagi give an awe-inspiring sense of Egypt, second only to being there, p67.

2 **Basilica di Superga** Reached by an original 1930s funicular, Turin's guardian angel is a baroque masterpiece, p60.

3 **Palazzo Reale and Palazzo Madama** These royal palaces of the house of Savoy were the seat of the dukes who presided over Turin for centuries, p34 and p37.

4 **Galleria d'Arte Moderna** A collection of seminal works from avant-garde and post-modernist art movements, p84.

5 **Galleria Sabauda** The Savoys' collection of old masters includes masterpieces by famous hands, from local Piemontese to the great Italian and Flemish masters, p65.

6 **La Mole Antonelliana and Museo Nazionale del Cinema** Spectacular views plus the best and most amusingly interactive cinema museum in Europe, p49.

7 **Il Duomo** Guarino Guarini's cathedral and in particularly the kaleidoscopical dome interior is a truly spiritual place, as befits the location of the famous Turin Shroud, p44.

8 **Museo della Santa Sindone** The Turin Shroud is one of the great enigmas of the world. This admirably impartial museum displays a replica as well as chapter and verse on the arguments and scientific research to date, p45.

9 **Il Lingotto** An icon of Turin's 20th-century industrial history, formerly the Fiat factory with a famous rooftop testing track, now a multi-faceted expo space, p78

10 **Val d'Aosta** An entrancing alpine setting with top-class skiing, Mont Blanc and the Matterhorn, p113.

The ★ symbol is used throughout this guide to indicate recommended sights.

Trip planner

From April through to October, Turin enjoys the typically balmy Mediterranean climate that will not disappoint visitors in search of hot, outdoor Italian life. August can be uncomfortably hot and many bars, restaurants and museums are closed so a visit during this month should be avoided. Winter is an altogether different proposition. From November to March Turin can be bitingly cold, although it rarely actually snows in the city, and the city is either sparkling under alpine sunshine or shrouded in a thick and magical fog which hangs around for days. Perhaps these months reveal the true colours of Turin. They are also the prime months for those wanting to use the city as a gateway to the mountains: snow is abundant from November sometimes until as late as mid-May.

A day

If you're only in Turin for 24 hours you'll need to be focused about what's important. If it's art, then go for overload at the Museo Egizio, Galleria Sabauda and Galleria d'Arte Moderna. If it's architecture, have a stroll round the baroque splendour of piazza Castello and head south for Renzo Piano's Lingotto and the Palazzo a Vela. For shopping, don't stray from via Roma. Or to soak up the rhythms of Italy, head for one of Turin's famous cafés, like the *Bicerin* or *Caffe San Carlo* and then seek out the aperitif haunts of the Murazzi and quadrilatero in the evening.

A long weekend

For many, a weekend visit to Italy is simply a case of lounging in bars, soaking up the country's distinct rhythm and moving from cappuccino to cappuccino. Time should be devoted to sampling the erudite literary atmosphere of the cafés in piazza San Carlo. If you want to justify this indulgence with a few bare bones of culture most of the main sites are within easy reach of each other.

Themed breaks

From piazza Castello the shortest of circuits could provide a trip through Turin's **regal history**, including a peep at Juvarra's scissor staircase and the luxurious rooms inside the Palazzo Reale, and the beautiful dome of Guarini's cathedral next door. Shroud hunters should visit the Museo della Santa Sindone to see the replica. Follow this with a visit to the underground tunnels and the Pietro Micca staircase on the site of the city's former citadel around via Cernaia.

Art lovers should not miss the the Museo Egizio, Galleria Sabauda and Galleria d'Arte Moderna, or a concert at the renowned Regio. A visit to the Mole Antonelliana is a must for film fans who will enjoy the building's innovative Museo Nazionale del Cinema in the city that is regarded as the birthplace of Italian cinema, see box, p51.

Shopaholics will find all the style they need to have their credit cards burning down the via Roma. For serious flea market junkies, *Il Gran Balon* on the second weekend of the month around Porta Palazzo is unmissable, while the weekly market in piazza Repubblica is sure to whet the appetite and satisfy lovers of Italian leather goods. See also p189.

A stroll down via Po and along the banks of the river in the parco Valentino provides a romantic route for **lovers** inspired by the spirit of Italy as will the hillside gardens and villas across the river. The Basilica di Superga is a favourite nocturnal haunt for lovers' trysts.

Turin is the capital of the Italian car. **Motor enthusiasts** should not miss Renzo Piano's conversion of the Lingotto Fiat factory and the nearby Museo dell'Automobile. A trip up the funicular to the Basilica di Superga is a good Sunday excursion for adults and children alike.

And then there is always **football** if either Juventus or Torino FC are playing at home. Tickets can be obtained at the stadium, at major newspaper kiosks and from the club websites and are easily available apart from for local derbies and European games. League games, in general, are sleepy affairs with a high level of skill, cat and mouse tactics and an emphasis on defence known as *catenaccio*. Not to mention those particular Italian quirks of shirt-pulling, long hair and flamboyant diving. See also Sport, p199.

A week or more

A longer visit will, in addition to the above, also allow time to linger a while in the city's more secretive spots such as in the medieval streets of the quadrilatero and to relax at greater length in the parco Valentino, perhaps taking in a visit to the Exhibition Halls and the fake medieval castle at its heart. There will be time to mess about on the river in rowing boats or canoes and also to cross the river Po and explore the green hills and parkland that rise above the city. A longer visit will also allow time to visit the fortress of Moncalieri and the majestic hunting lodge of Stupinigi to the south of the city as well the other royal lodges and castles peppered around the outskirts of the city.

Depending on the season, visitors with more time should take the chance to head out either northwest to the Alps and the Aosta Valley, ablaze with flowers and beautiful walking trails in spring and offering a wide choice of ski resorts during winter. Under an hour's drive east of the city are the world-famous vineyards of the Barolo and Barbera wines, a region of picturesque hilltop villages, guardians of local Italian traditions, and guarantor of fine wining and dining, especially in October when the hunt begins for the prized white truffle.

Contemporary Turin

Turin's past, the baroque splendour of its royal architecture and its stately Parisian hauteur, was defined by the dukes of Savoy, but the city's 20th century was defined by a different, more modern aristocracy, the Agnelli Dynasty, founders of the Fabbrica Italiana Automobili Torino – FIAT. At the end of the 19th century it was the Agnellis that ensured Turin, divested of the mantle of Italy's capital, maintained a major role in the newly founded country, reinventing itself as an industrial powerhouse at the apex of the so-called industrial triangle with Milan and Genoa.

Turin's industrial importance shaped much of what the city was to become. In promoting the car, Turin – the engine, literally, of Italy – celebrated the very values that were central to the artists and architects of the early 20th century avant-garde movements being theorized further afield in Paris: the new, the fast and the marriage of design with function. The grand city of arcades and palazzi had to expand and adapt to its new vocation and some of the buildings that sprung up in those early decades, such as the Lingotto factory, praised by Filippo Marinetti, founder of Futurism, as a masterpiece, are not merely the simple industrial spaces they appear but important pieces of a modernist architectural legacy. Turin was the first Italian city to import modernist influences into the country and, due to its proximity and historic openness to French influence, it was the city that imported many of the vogues, fashions and movements that had their origin in the French capital: art nouveau architecture, Parisian fashion and cinema.

As with many industrial cities worldwide, Turin is regenerating and reinventing its disused factories and warehouses. And, as elsewhere, these unusual spaces have found favour with the local artistic community, giving rise to a particularly fertile contemporary arts scene. It has become an important and prevalent feature of the cityscape, as the Galleria d'Arte Moderna (GAM) and plethora of city art galleries bear testimony.

Turin is the birthplace of Italian cinema, and to this day, far away from the studio world of Rome's Cinecitta and the glamour of the Venice festival, the city's yearly young film makers festival presides over the discovery and nurturing of the latest and brightest national and international talent. Turin was also the birthplace of Italian state radio and television network RAI, and also of Italian aviation. The city is currently the site of the biggest aeronautical and space factory design bureau in the country. So while various mantles have passed on to other more lauded cities, Turin should be remembered as a city of firsts.

Industry, and specifically mass car production, needed serious manpower and created thousands of jobs. In the 1950s and 1960s the promise of a job and northern riches attracted a mass immigration to Turin from Italy's south, an invited workforce similar to Germany's Turkish *gastarbeiter* even in so far as Italy's southerners are often viewed by those in the north as coming from another (poorer) country. Decades later immigration from southern Italy was followed by immigration from northern Africa. It has been a continual process that has changed the face of Turin, at once creating the medium-rise suburban sprawl to the north and south but also transforming the genetic and cultural make-up of its population in a modern expression of the city's historic openness to outside and foreign influence. Unusual among Italian metropoles, Turin is both multicultural and racially integrated, and its cultural and in particular music scene has profited from this welcoming attitude. As the clubs of the Murazzi under the arches by the river Po testify, Turin is a hive of African-based rhythms, producing local bands such as Mau Mau, Africa United and Subsonica that have become international success stories with their own unique brand of Italian roots reggae and break beats.

In these clubs you will find a subversive culture that is not what you might expect of modern Italian youth. It turns out to be the norm in Turin. For Turin is not, like Milan or Florence, an expression of the flash beautiful-on-the-outside designer Italy that has become

★ **Dizzy heights**
Antonelli's extraordinary spear, la Mole Antonelliana, was once the tallest brick building in the world

the national stereotype, parading around in sunglasses, Armani suits and Gucci loafers. Turin is more a leather jackets, raw, scruffy and slightly hippy city that has its roots firmly in an honest, worker mentality. These are the children of a strong anti-capitalist heritage. Just as in Turin's 19th-century cafés the idea of an Italian constitution was spawned devolving governmental power from the monarch, so in the early 20th-century Turin, the Italian Trade Union movement was formed on the FIAT factory floors and with it, under the leadership of Antonio Gramsci, the Italian Communist Party (PCI). Contemporary Italian politics may be totally dominated by the Milanese ex-crooner, Berlusconi and the PCI struggling for an identity as credible opposition but Turin as a city has always represented the opposite pole. Until his recent death, the much-loved Gianni Agnelli, President of Fiat, nicknamed l'Avvocato (the lawyer), was the sole national figurehead of this opposition. He represented honest blue-collar sweat versus il Seduttore's white-collar sleaze and spin; historic Juventus against the nouveau riche of AC Milan; his newspaper La Stampa a critical independent voice.

Turin does not evoke traditional romantic visions of Italy. It has never sought the limelight and if anything has benefited from being eclipsed. It remains an unconventional city, different from and less superficial than much of Italy and as contemporary as London or Berlin. Now that truffles, Barolo wine and the 2006 Winter Olympic stage have alerted the tourist industry to her treasures, it may seem as if Turin has roused herself from a deep post-industrial hangover. Long before the 2006 Winter Olympic mantle was bestowed on her, she was already beginning to have fun and make the most of her strange collection of assets, all the time without losing her royal demeanour. Turin is still the car capital of Italy and, like a classic Pininfarina design, she has beautiful lines. And where in Birmingham or Detroit could you look up at the end of a long boulevard and set eyes on the distant white crown of the Alps?

Turin can be reached very easily and economically from the UK, with regular flights departing daily from Stansted direct to the city's Caselle airport. Turin is also set to be linked by the Eurostar service arriving from Geneva and going on to Milan. Within the city, Turin's network of efficient trams and buses provides dependable and cheap access to all corners of the city. A single-line underground is under construction but is not due to be finished until 2006. Most of the central sites are close to each other and linked by arcaded boulevards so pedestrians will find Turin a pleasant place to navigate on foot, although public transport is recommended for sites down the seemingly endless boulevards to the south.

Getting there

Air

From UK and the rest of Europe **Ryanair** flies daily from Stansted to Turin's Sandro Pertini airport, commonly referred to as Caselle after the village it is near. The direct flight takes just under two hours. Watch out for special offers for flights at a derisory £0.09 pence each way (not including taxes of £13.26 outbound and £8.82 return), so you can get there and back from as little as £22.17. There is a small discount for booking online at www.ryanair.com. **British Airways** flies direct to Turin from London Gatwick with two flights daily, from £88.30 return including taxes. The Italian national carrier **Alitalia** and its competitors, **Air One** and **Meridiana** offer scheduled services connecting the UK. Other airlines such as **Lufthansa** and **Iberia** offer non-direct services via Stuttgart and Madrid respectively. Otherwise Turin is connected by direct scheduled flights to most major European capitals. Useful alternatives to bear in mind are **Ryanair** flights to Genoa (just over an hour by train) and a greater choice of scheduled services to Milan (1hr 40 mins by train). In addition to the above, a number of charter airlines such as **Monarch**, **Britannia** and **Air 2000** offer occasional and seasonal services to Turin from Birmingham and Manchester and London Gatwick airports. For more details contact flight information at Caselle airport, **T** 011 5675 361/2.

From North America There are no direct flights to Turin from the USA or Canada. The best and cheapest option is to fly to London (US$5-600 off season, up to US$1,000 during summer) and take an onward connection from there or to fly direct to Milan and take one of the regular good-value intercity trains from Milan to Turin.

From Australia and New Zealand There are currently no direct flights to any Italian destination from Australia or New Zealand.

➜ Airlines and travel agents

Alitalia www.alitalia.it
Air France www.airfrance.com
Air One www.air-one.it
British Airways www.ba.com
Meridiana www.meridiana.it
Ryanair www.ryanair.com
Expedia www.expedia.com
Travelocity www.travelocity.com
Last Minute www.lastminute.com
STA Travel www.sta-travel.com
Trailfinders www.trailfinders.com

The best option is to fly to an alternative European hub (such as London , Amsterdam, Frankfurt) and take an onward connection; alternatively head for Milan and then connect by train to Turin.

Airport information

Turin's Sandro Pertini Airport, commonly referred to as Caselle, **T** 011 5676 6361/2, www.turin-airport.com, lies 16 km due north of Turin near the town of Caselle. It is a small, modern with one terminal for all departures and arrivals, a good information bureau and facilities for money exchange and withdrawal, car hire and a small bar and restaurant. There is not a vast selection of shops inside the airport. See also Directory, p215 for airport information.

The journey from the airport to the city centre takes about 30 minutes by car. A taxi for a one-way trip costs around € 25. Taxis can be found immediately outside the arrivals hall. The airport taxi number is **T** 011 996 3090, for others, see Getting Around below.

The new train service into Turin's Dora station is reliable and takes 30 mins. From the airport to Turin, the service departs twice hourly at 19 and 49 minutes past the hour; from Turin to the airport , again twice hourly at 13 and 43 minutes past the hour. Tickets cost € 2.58 each way. Further information on this link can be obtained from **T** 011 6910000, www.gtt.to.it

A bus connection to the city centre runs between 0515-2300. Between 0515-0745 the bus leaves every 30 minutes at 15 and 45 past; between 0815-1545 every 45 mins; between 1630-2030 every 30 mins, and between 2100-2230 every 45 mins again. Tickets can be purchased on board, in newstands or at the bus terminal at either end and cost € 5 each way for the 40-minute journey. Stops in town include both Turin's main railway stations, Porta Susa and Porta Nuova, also the journey's terminus at the corner of via Sacchi 8 and via Assietta. For more information contact **T** 011 3000611.

Car
The recently reopened Mont Blanc tunnel has long ensured that Turin was well-connected by road to countries north of the Alps. As far as Aosta the road used to be long and winding but now the A5 motorway has halved the journey time. The A4 motorway between Turin and Milan is one of Italy's most congested by commuter traffic and peak times (7-9am and 4-7pm) are to be avoided. Tolls are payable on all Italian motorways and for the Mont Blanc tunnel but the more scenic SS (*strade statali*) are free. EU nationals with their own vehicles need an international insurance certificate, also known as a *carta verde* (green card). For more information contact *Automobile Club Italiano* in Rome on **T** 06 49981, 24 hrs. In case of emergency breakdown call **T** 116. Traffic news is available from *Societa Autostrade* **T**06 43632121, www.infoviabilita.it, or by radio on FM 103.3.

Coach
Masochists, or those on a very strict budget, can go by coach from London to Turin, taking roughly 24 hours. *Eurolines UK* runs the service which departs from London's Victoria coach station **T** 08705 143219, www.gobycoach.com or www.eurolines.com

→ **Torino card**

One of the most important investments you can make to get the most out of the city in a short space of time is the Torino card. Costing € 15 for 48 hours and € 17 for 72 hours, the card allows free unlimited use of the city's public transport system (including the train up to Superga and the Mole Antonelliana panoramic life), free entry into over 120 museums, free trips on the TurismoBus and Po river boat cruises and discounts of up to 50% on theatre tickets, guided tours, bike hire and cinema admission. Torino cards are on sale at the tourist information office and in selected hotels.

Train

Turin has three stations, Porta Nuova, **T** 011 5613333, the grandiose terminus station in the heart of the city serving all destinations; Porta Susa, **T** 011 538513, to the west for the Aosta valley and destinations northwest of the city, and the small station of Dora, **T** 011 221 7835, the terminus of the airport rail link. Grand old Porta Nuova will in time be sidelined and Porta Susa will become the principal station in Turin with the advent of the Eurostar link. This is still some way off – the work should be completed for the 2006 Winter Olympics – and at the time of going to press Porta Nuova was still Turin main rail nexus, but times and destinations will increasingly vary.

Either way, Turin is a major junction on Italy's much hugely efficient and good value rail network. By train the city is connected to Paris (4 hrs) and Milan (1hr 40 mins) and by extension to many European destinations. Fares are charged by the kilometre so there are no intricate fare systems for apex super-saver returns and the like. Tickets must be date-stamped by one of the machines on the station platform before travel. There are various types of train, each basically an indicator of speed with the *diretto*, *espresso* and *inter-regionale* stopping more frequently and the *IC* (Intercity) trains whisking you direct and requiring a supplement. For

comprehensive fares and timetable information contact TrenItalia
T 011 892 021/199 166177 (from within Italy) www.trenitalia.com.

Getting around

Turin is quite a long city, characterized by seemingly endless
avenues but thankfully most of the main sights are within an easy
and safe 20 minutes of each other. The network of trams and buses
is generally excellent and good value and subject to quite regular
flash strikes, although usually not at weekends.

Bicycle and vespa
Turin is not one of Italy's most bicycle-friendly cities. Nor has it
taken to the vespa in the same way as other Italian cities. That said,
both represent a good if hair-raising way of getting around the
city. See Directory, p216 for hire shops for bicycles and vespas.

Bus and tram
From 0500-0000 Turin is served by a very efficient network of
buses and trams, from rickety old post-war survivors to
ultra-modern trams and alternative fuel-powered buses. These are
run by the **Azienda Torinese Mobilita**(ATM), **T** 800019152,
www.atm.to.it and a detailed map of line numbers and routes is
available from their sales office in the Porta Nuova atrium. Tickets
are transferable between bus and tram and can be bought at a city
outlet (bar or newsagent) furnishing the 'T' (Tabacchi) sign outside.
An *ordinario* costs € 0.90 and is valid 70 mins from the time you
punch it in the machines on board. A carnet of 15 tickets costs
€ 12.50. There is also a *giornaliero* daily card which costs € 3 and is
valid all day; a shopping ticket costing € 1.80 and valid for four
hours between 0900-2000 and the group card, *viaggiare insieme*,
€ 4 , valid for up to four people between 1430-2000 on Saturdays
and public holidays. All tickets are valid for travel anywhere in the
city within the allotted time.

→ Car hire

Avis at airport **T** 011 4701528; on C.so Turati 37, **T** 011 501107; at Porta Nuova **T** 011 6699800, www.avis.com

Europcar via Madama Cristina 72, **T** 011 6503603; at airport **T** 011 5678048; at Porta Nuova **T** 011 6502066, www.europcar.com

Hertz at airport **T** 011 5678166; on via Magellano **T** 011 502080, www.hertz.com

Maggiore at airport **T** 011 4701929; on C.so Moncalieri 217 **T** 011 6614629; at Porta Nuova, **T** 011 6503013

Sixt at airport **T** 011 4702381; on via Madama Cristina 111/c **T** 011 5678090, www.sixt.com

Targarent at airport T 011 5678090; via Nizza 43, T 011 655685. Normal EU driving rules apply: you must be over 18 with all car papers with you to hire a car. No international license is required.

Car

Ironically, Turin has become steadily less car-friendly in recent years in an attempt to alleviate the pollution problems that the general absence of wind in the city does not allow to dissipate. Driving is not recommended in the city due to excessive traffic and a lack of parking spaces. The area between piazza Statuto and piazza Castello is banned to all private vehicles without a permit between 0730-1030. There are also frequent directives allowing only cars with certain number plates to circulate, again to alleviate pollution. There are numerous car parks and almost every street in the centre is now metered. The website www.comune.torino.it has details of all car-related restrictions.

Coach

Within Italy Turin is well-connected by the national bus (Pullman) network of blue coaches allowing easy and regular access to the Ligurian Riviera, the Val d'Aosta and Milan. Two companies cover the regio, **SATTI** (**T** 800990097) and **SADEM** (**T** 011 433 2525), the first for the northern region and the latter further afield. **SADEM**'s station is on the corner of via Castelfidardo and C.so Vittorio Emanuele II while **SATTI**'s main station is on via Fiochetto 23. For general bus enquiries look up www.italybus.it

Taxi
In Italy it is not customary to hail taxis in the street. The taxi network runs either by going to the nearest taxi rank or by calling one of the city's taxi co-operative numbers: **T** 011 5737, **T** 011 5730 or **T** 011 3399. You will be charged for the time/distance it takes to come to you pick-up point plus the subsequent fare. There may also be additional charges for the airport, luggage etc. Have change ready as Italian taxi drivers have a miraculous knack of not having any if it means they can round up the fare. There is also a disabled taxi service available on **T** 011 58116.

La Metropolitana
Construction is already well underway for Turin's underground railway, to be completed by 2006. There will be just one line initially running on a north-south axis through the city and connecting the centre and factory districts with the outlying countryside. The plan is that as transport is taken underground, some of Turin's major arteries, such as Corso Vittorio Emanuele, will become leafy pedestrian boulevards with fountains, sculptures and cycle paths.

Tours

An aerial view
The observation point at the top of the Mole Antonelliana is reached by the funky *ascensore panoramico* lift inside the tower. Tickets cost € 3.62 euros. From here you can enjoy 360-degree views of the city, the Alps and surrounding wine regions.

Boat tours

Two boats, the Valentino and the Valentina ply the serene waters of the river Po all summer (and in winter only on public holidays) departing from the quay down by the Murazzi at the edge of piazza Vittorio Veneto. There are three routes. The first (€ 2.07) includes a visit to the fake Medieval castle in the parco Valentino; the second (€ 4.13) has a trip to the exhibition halls further south in the park; the third (€ 5.16) runs as far as Moncalieri. By tickets on board, at the Murazzi quay or in the Valentino Medieval Castle.

Bus tours

Bus tours are run by **TurismoBus Torino**, between the hours of 1000-1900, all summer from July to mid-September and over the Christmas and New Year period. Tours depart every hour and take in all the main sites of interest and also the most beautiful roads. You can get off at any of the 14 stops and then rejoin the tour on the next bus. Tours cost € 6 per person and can be purchased at the tourist information office on piazza Castello, at the airport or in Porta Nuova station, also in hotels and various travel agents.

Funicular to the Superga

The funicular railway up to the Basilica of the Superga was built in 1884. A quaint 1930s wooden tram now takes you up to the basilica with beautiful vistas towards the alps and over the city. The tram departs from the Stazione Sassi on piazza Modena which you can reach by tram number 15. Tickets cost € 3.10 for a single, € 4.13 for a return and it is free if you have a Torino Card, see p24.

Walking tours

Turismotorino also offer themed guided walking tours (museums, black magic etc) costing € 6 per person and running from April to January. **T** 011 535901/535181 for bookings. Tours are to be had in a variety of languages including English, French, German and Spanish.

→ Travel extras

Safety Turin is generally a safe and well-lit city. However, it is best to avoid being on your own at night around piazza Repubblica, the Murazzi and in the little roads west of via Nizza around the station. Women will receive the attention of the unveiled Latin gaze, but this should be seen as flattery and nothing more.

Tipping Generous tipping, around 10-15%, is the norm.

Vaccinations No special vaccinations are required.

Visas Holders of EC, US, Canadian, Australian and New Zealand passports do not need a visa for entry into Italy.

Tourist information

Turin's **main tourist office** is located at Atrium in the centre of piazza Solferino, **T** 011 535181, **F** 011 530070. There is also an office in piazza Castello inside the Palazzo Madama, **T** 011 535901, on arrival at the **airport**, **T** 011 5678124, and in the Porta Nuova station, **T** 011 531327. The official website www.turismotorino.org has details in English, as does www.comune.torino.it. For further information about the city in Italian, consult www.a-torino.com, www.torino.vivacity.it and www.torinocultura.it

---

Tourist offices outside Turin

Alba
piazza Medford, **T** 0173 35833, *Tue-Fri 0900-1200, 1530-1830, Sat 0900-1200*. Well-supplied with maps and information on the surrounding area, including accommodation options and details of wine makers. See also p107.

Asti

piazza Alfieri, **T** 0141 530 357, *Mon-Fri 0900-1230, 1500-1800, closed Sat pm*. A good selection of maps and information on the Palio horserace and accommodation options. See also p109.

Val d'Susa

C.so Inghilterra 39, Susa, **T** 0122 622470; in **Sestriere**, via Pinerolo 14, **T** 0122 755444. All offices have information on snow conditions, ski, walking and biking trails, as well as accommodation and eating options in the area. See also p110.

Saluzzo

via Griselda 6, **T** 0175 46710, *Mon-Fri 0830-1230, 1430-1530*. Information on tours, opening hours and maps of the whole Saluzzo valley region. See also p111.

The Val d'Aosta

piazza Chanoux 8, Aosta, **T** 0165 236627, daily 0900-1300, 1500-2000, closed Sunday pm Oct-May. In **Courmayeur**, **T** 0165 842060 and **Cervinia**, **T** 0166 949136. The *Societa Guide Alpine di Courmayeur*, piazzale Monte Bianco, **T** 0165 842064, has specific information on mountaineering trails in this area. See also p113.

Ivrea

C.so Vercelli 1, **T** 0125 618131, **F** 0125 618140, daily 0930-1230, 1430-1830, www.canavese-vallilanzo.it For information on sleeping, transport, restaurants, the nearby area and carnival. See also p115.

The Centre – Royal Turin

Although not necessarily the fulcrum of contemporary torinese life, **piazza Castello** *is its most important square. The architectural imprints etched on this historic area trace the city's political history through the reign of the House of Savoy and the founding of the Italian state. Set at the confluence of via Po, via Roma and via Pietro Micca, the square is enclosed by a fortress of baroque façades and colonnades such as the* **Palazzo Reale** *(Royal Palace), the* **Armeria Reale, Segreteria di Stato** *and* **Archivio di Stato**. *This was the so-called* Zona di Comando, *the command zone, of the Savoy dukes, a complex of galleries, passageways and interconnecting offices of power designed so that they would not have to expose themselves to the public. At the square's centre is the* **Palazzo Madama**, *the castle from which the square takes its name and which now contains one of the city's main art collections in the* **Museo Civico di Arte Antica**. *Behind the Palazzo Reale are the* **Giardini Reali**, *the royal gardens, while annexed to the palace is Turin's* **cathedral** *whose beautiful chapel used to house the* **Turin Shroud**. *South of piazza Castello the elegance of designer Italy stretches down* **via Roma**, *the city's catwalk and most dark blue address culminating in the arcaded and honey-coloured square of* **piazza San Carlo**, *once the hub of Turin's fierce political and intellectual café life.*

▸▸ *See Sleeping p123, Eating and drinking p143.*

◉ Sights

Piazza Castello
Map 2, C 6-7, p252-253

Piazza Castello reflects perfectly the three architectural phases of central Turin's development and expansion. The first plans were laid in 1587 by the architect Ascanio Vitozzi at the behest of the

Savoy King, Carlo Emmanuele I. Vitozzi is thought responsible for the arcaded buildings that line the western side of the square. Architect Amedeo Castellamonte completed the square in the 17th century but it is the flourishes and eye for the grandiose of Filippo Juvarra (1678-1736) whose impact really endures to this day. As the political fulcrum of the city, it was known as 'la culla del Risorgimento' (the cradle of Italian Unity). No doubt due to the Savoys' origins, proximity to France and also the prevailing trend of the time, there is something of the feel of a French chateau to the square and the atmosphere could easily be deemed more imperial Parisian than flamboyant Italian. Until only recently the square was in fact a more typically Italian swirl of cars and scooters and featured heavily in the famous traffic jam in the film, *The Italian Job*. It has since been partially pedestrianized and those parts given over to fountains and *passeggiatas*.

★ Palazzo Madama

piazza Castello, **T** 011 4429931, www.comune.torino.it/ palazzomadama *Tue-Fri and Sun 1000-2000, Sat 1000-2300. Mon closed. Entry to hall is free.* Map 2, C7, p253

An architectural cocktail of contrasting eras and styles the centrepiece to piazza Castello is a synthesis of the story of Turin. Although not visible from outside, the two front columns behind the façade are the remains of the Porta Praetoria, one of the gates in the walls of the Roman settlement of Giulia Augusta Taurinorum founded in 28 BC. In the 13th century the gate was transformed into a castle using the red-brick which characterizes the main body of the building. Later in the 13th century the city fell definitively under Savoy rule and in the 15th century a nobleman, Ludovico d'Acaia, transformed it from a fortress to a ducal palace. The name 'Madama' refers to two women ('madama' being piemontese for 'lady'): firstly, Maria Cristina of France, the wife of Duke Vittorio Amedeo, and subsequently, Maria Giovanna Battista of Savoie-Nemours, the second wife of Duke Carlo Emmanuele II. While the red-brick mass is rather lumpy and ivy-ridden, the highlight of the Palazzo Madama is the baroque façade designed by Filippo Juvarra and built between 1718-21. The façade was part of a much more ambitious project that was never completed. Inside, Juvarra's beautiful staircase sweeps up from the entrance to an upper hall, fit for a ballroom sequence from a Visconti film but instead desecrated by Michael Caine's minis in *The Italian Job*. A tunnel used to link the Palazzo Madama to the Palazzo Reale but this was destroyed during the Franco-Spanish siege at the turn of the 19th century. Thereafter the castle served many functions: the royal art gallery, an astronomical observatory and importantly as the seat of the newly-formed Italian Senate from 1848-60 and the Italian Senate from 1861-64. Since 1934, the Turin city council has shared the building with the city's large collection of antiquities and fine art, currently closed while the palace is under restoration. In front of the castle are three statues: the first, directly in front, dedicated to the ensign of the army of the King of Sardinia; the second, to the south, dedicated to the Italian cavalry, and the more easterly monument to Emanuele Filiberto, Duca d'Aosta.

Museo Civico d'Arte Antica

Palazzo Madama, piazza Castello, **T** 011 4429931. *Currently closed for restoration. Map 2, C7, p253*

The museum is currently closed for restoration (due to re-open in 2006) and for now, it is only possible to admire Juvarra's staircase and atrium. However, when it does open it will display an appetizing collection of paintings, sculptures, altarpieces and figurines by Piemontese masters as well as stained glass, ceramics, enamels, prints and drawings. There are a number of notable highlights: the *Portrait of a Man* by Antonello da Messina (1476), the *Desana Horde* of 47 Ostrogothic artefacts in gold and silver and the *Heures de Milan* book the *Heures de Milan* book (full title: *Les tres riches heures du duc Berry*) with illustrations by Jan van Eyck and his

▶ The House of Savoy

Equally as important, if not as ferocious as Italy's other famous ruling families, the dukes of Savoy reigned over Piedmont and Turin for over 500 years. Of French origin, they remained closely linked to France by marriage with French royalty.

That said, their heart remained with, and in defense of, their Piemontese realm and their capital city Chambery. The lineage began with Umberto I Biancamano and the marriage in 1046 of his son to Adelaide of Susa, the marquess of Turin. Following him were Amedeo VI, the so-called *Conte Verde*, Amedeo VII, the *Conte Rosso* and Amedeo VIII, the *Pacifico*, who was made duke of the realm in 1416. This era is subject of much legend and historical conjecture. It is only with Emanuele Filiberto who ruled from 1553-80 that the historical thread can be picked up. He transferred the capital of the realm from Chambery to Turin in 1563 and set about the annexation of the surrounding city-states into the Savoy dukedom.

It was under Vittorio Amedeo I (1630-37), his son, Carlo Emanuele II (1638-75) and their respective Queens, Maria Cristina of France and Maria Giovanna Battista di Savoia-Nemours, that the city began to blossom. Vittorio Amedeo II (1684-1732) was the first to gain the title King via the war of Spanish succession, first of all in 1713 as King of Sicily and then in 1720 as King of Sardinia. Then came Vittorio Emanuele I (1802- 21), followed by his son, Carlo Felice (1821-31). At this point Carlo Alberto (1831- 49) of the next remove in line, the Savoy-Carignano, rose to the throne.

His son, Vittorio Emanuele II presided over the founding of Italy and gained the name, 'Padre della Patria'. He was the first King of Italy. The reign of the Savoy Dynasty came to an end in 1946 with Umberto II and the declaration of the Italian Republic.

school. The museum is also famous for the decoration of its rooms by Domenico Guidobono in 18th century, in particular the depictions of the four seasons, his Chinese study and the museum's northwest terrace.

★ Palazzo Reale

piazza Castello, piazzetta Reale, piazza Castello, **T** 011 436 1455, www.ambienteto.arti.beniculturali.it *Tue-Sun 0900-1930. € 6.50, free with Torino Card. Map 2, C6, p252*

The Palazzo Reale, Turin's Buckingham Palace, is the main focus of the piazza Castello and the architectural ledger par excellence of the city's royal history. The palace occupies half the northern side of the piazza and is linked by interconnecting corridors and passages to the former royal state buildings to the right and to the cathedral and chapel to the left. There is an undoubtable touch of Paris about the grand entrance flanked by the two equestian statues of Castor and Pollux but the façade, with its squat towers at either end, is more reminiscent of a grand Italian country villa. Recently repainted and restored to its Savoy light blue-grey, the 107-m façade by Amedeo di Castellemonte is in fact the only original piece of the palace complex left, the rest being influenced and changed by subsequent centuries and architects. The idea of a royal palace formed part of Ascanio Vitozzi's 1584 plan for the centre of Turin. Commissioned by Carlo Emanuele II, work began in 1646 on the site of the old bishop's palace. The initial construction was completed in 14 years and was the home of the House of Savoy until 1865. The interior truly bears the stamp of royalty. It has a birthday cake of chandeliers and a sequence of rooms with heraldic names such as La Sala delle Vittorie and La Sala delle Dignita, furnished with Chinese vases, sculptures, paintings, frescos, gold leaf and coffered ceilings. They conserve and display the work of the great artists practising in Turin between the 17th and 19th centuries: Jan Miel, Daniel Seyter, Filippo Juvarra, Francesco Beaumont and Pelagio Palagi. It was Juvarra who

★ **Baroque and roll**
Juvarra's baroque staircase in Palazzo Madama.

contributed the masterpiece for which the Palazzo Reale is most famous – the amazing architectural feat of the Scala delle Forbici (Scissor Staircase), so-called due to its ornate criss-cross design. It was designed in anticipation of the arrival of the bride of Carlo Emanuele III, Anna Christina of Bavaria and heralds a sequence of glorious reception rooms and private apartments. Among these are the Galleria del Daniel, the ballroom named after the beautiful vaults painted by the Viennese artist, Daniel Seyter, and the Galleria Beaumont (which houses the Armeria Reale) refurbished in the 18th century under Benedetto Alfieri. Of the 40 rooms it is only possible to visit those on the first floor, including the private apartments of Carlo Alberto, Queen Maria Teresa and the magnificent main ballroom supported by 20 columns and with a capacity for over 200 guests.

I Giardini Reali

Winter 0800-1900, summer 0800-1600. Entry free although there are plans to charge in the immediate future. Map 2, B7-8, p253.

Accessed through the arcaded courtyard behind the Palazzo Reale, the Savoys' royal gardens were landscaped very much in the French style by Andre Le Notre, also the designer of gardens at Versailles, between 1697-98. Enclosed within the fortifications of the palace complex, they feature grassy ramparts, multiple statues and a kaleidoscope of flowerbeds. At the centre is a fountain with a mythological grouping by Simone Martinez from 1750. They are unmissable, particularly for those who are less interested in interior design.

Armeria Reale

piazza Castello 191, **T** 011 543889, www.artito.beniculturali.it *Tue, Thu, Sat, Sun 1330-1930, Wed, Fri 0830-1400. Closed Mon. € 4. Part of the palace complex on the north side of piazza Castello to the right of Palazzo Reale.* Map 2, C7, p253

The former armoury of the Savoy kings forms part of the impressive palace complex. The armoury was transformed into a public museum by Carlo Alberto in 1837 having commissioned Vittorio Seyssel d'Aix to collect and catalogue arms from the arsenals of Turin and Genoa. The collection subsequently expanded in the 19th century through acquisition and now represents one of the most important collections of arms in Europe. The contents of the armoury is one thing, but its setting is quite another. The three rooms on the first floor at the top of the grand staircase by Benedetto Alfieri are spectacular, richly furnished with sculptures and stucco work. La Sala della Rotonda, a former ballroom, was designed by Pelagio Palagi while the Galleria Beaumont was desgined by Juvarra and finished by Alfieri. Francesco Beaumont painted the beautiful depictions of *Stories of Aeneas* in the vaults. Showcased in these rooms are arms from the Italian and German schools of the 15th and 16th centuries, including the cavalry arms of Emanuele Filiberto and Ascanio Maria Sforza from the end of 15th century. The collection features daggers, stilettos (a type of Italian dagger), spears, swords and firearms of all shapes and sizes, including a number of Napoleonic swords and arms from the Garibaldi era. Thematically, the museum covers the story of weaponry from prehistory to the First World War, also taking in arms from Turkey, the Caucasus, Persia and the Far East.

La Biblioteca Reale

piazza Castello, **T** 011 543855   *Only open for temporary exhibitions.* *Map 2, C7, p253*

On the ground floor of the same wing of the palace as the Armeria Reale is Turin's royal library, located in a large rectangular hall designed by Pelagio Palagi. Founded by Carlo Alberto in 1831, the library is an impressive collection of some 200,000 volumes, including rare manuscripts, bookbindings and drawings. By far the most important piece of the collection, if not one of the great and little-known treasures of Turin, is the bearded self-portrait by Leonardo Da Vinci. It is sadly not on constant display but both this and his *Code on the Flight of Birds* (1505)are always available to be viewed on request.

L'Archivio di Stato

piazza Castello, **T** 011 540382 astoarchivio@multix.it *Only open for temporary exhibitions.* *Map 2, C7, p253*

Running across the northeastern side of piazza Castello, Turin's state archives occupy a building that incorporates the remains of the old Teatro Regio. Recently beautifully restored, it was designed by Filippo Juvarra and built between 1731-34. Inside are over 13 centuries of documentation of life and death in Turin. Even if you're not into medieval history, it's still worth a look for Juvarra's interior decoration.

Teatro Regio

piazza Castello 215, **T** 011 8815241. *Tue-Fri 1030-1800, Sat 1030-1600, Mon closed. For tickets and information contact www.teatroregio.torino.it* *Map 2, C7, p253*

Set under the classical arcades on the northeastern side, Turin's new royal theatre presents a contemporary façade of glass and metal. The old theatre, built in 1740 and designed by Benedetto Alfieri, was destroyed by fire in 1936. The new one, built to designs by Carlo Mollino and Marcello Zavelani Rossi, was inaugurated in 1973 and plays host to a calendar of prestigious operas and concerts. The Teatro Regio also houses a precious archive of musical documentation and witnessed the premieres of *Manon Lescaut* in 1893 and *La Bohème*, both by Puccini, in 1896.

! Primo Levi was born in Turin and lived on Corso Umberto 75. His tombstone in Turin bears his name, dates and his Auschwitz prisoner number 174517.

▶ **The Turin Shroud**

The most famous bedsheet in the world, alleged to be that in which the body of Jesus was wrapped after he was taken down from the cross, is Turin's most potent symbol. Debate has raged between the scientific and theological camps since scientific tests were first carried out in 1898. No test has proven anything conclusively since no results can be agreed on, including the carbon dating which placed the cloth in the Middle Ages, and so the mystery prevails. Sitting on the fence, Pope John Paul II deemed the cloth "useful for stimulating intelligent debate regarding the life of Jesus". Cyberspace has globalized the debate with overnight pundits and self-proclaimed experts setting up websites preaching their version as gospel. Whatever version, intelligence or legend you choose to believe, one fact is inescapable: the cloth, 437 cm long by 111 cm wide does contain the imprint, like a photographic negative of a man, 1,77 m tall who has been tortured and crucified.

Appropriately for an object so shrouded in mystery itself, how it came to reside in Turin is something of a detective novel. The first sign of its existence has been traced to Jerusalem in AD 33. The Shroud then pops up again in Constantinople in 944 and thereafter in France, at Lirey in 1353. It is supposed to have been given to the Savoy dukes by a French lady in 15th century whereafter it was kept in

Chiesa di San Lorenzo

piazzetta Reale, piazza Castello, **T** 011 4361527. *0800-1200, 1500-1900. At the entrance to the piazzetta Reale in the northwest corner of piazza Castello. Map 2, C6, p252*

The outwardly simple church of San Lorenzo contains many rich artistic details. The church was built on the site of an old church,

Chambery, capital of their dukedom, from 1453. Not counting the brief sojourn in Genoa to protect it from the Franco-Spanish invasions of 1706, the Shroud has resided in Turin since 1578.

The Shroud has had several narrow escapes, its survival each time adding weight to its mystic properties. In 1532 the Savoy castle in Chambery caught fire, but the Shroud was saved by the silver casket it was in except for a drop of molten silver which burnt a hole through the folded cloth. On its journey from Chambery to Turin it survived the onslaughts of various bands of robbers, and in 1581 the French tried to steal the Shroud, only to find it had disappeared, reappearing only when the aggressors had fled. The Shroud has been connected with many a miracle, apparition, enigma and prophecy, the latest of which was its survival in the fire of April 1997. The Shroud is now kept in the left-hand transept of the cathedral behind bullet-proof glass. It lies flat in an aluminium box in a vacuum and covered in damask cloth against damage from the light.

After the death of the last would-be King of Italy, Umberto, in 1983, the Shroud passed, by Umberto's own will, out of the hands of the Savoy and into those of the Pope. It makes very few public appearances, the latest being in 1978, 1998 and 2000. It will not be on display again until 2025.

Santa Maria del Presepe, to fulfil a vow made by Emanuele Filiberto on the eve of the Battle of San Quintino on 10 August 1557. The church has an octagonal plan modelled on the Greek cross topped by a famous and ingenious baroque dome by Guarini composed of interwoven arches. Belied by its simple exterior, which is generally believed to be unfinished, the inside of San Lorenzo is a feast of the baroque with colours and detail sparkling from sculptures, paintings, stucco work, coloured marble and gilding. Of the many altars the most spectacular is the high altar by Guarini himself which is adorned with a bas-relief by Carlo Antonio Tantardini depicting Duke Emanuele's vow. The pulpit is a beautiful piece of carving as are the stalls with inlaid panels and the organ has an unusually decorative loft. The current aspect of the church and its interior was not finally reached until 1880.

Palazzo Chiablese

piazza San Giovanni 2. *Closed to the public except for special events.*
Map 2, C6, p252

The Chiablese palace forms the left side of the piazzetta Reale, the forecourt to the main Royal Palace. Inside it is connected to the apartments of the Royal Palace and it was here that Benedetto Maurizio, Duca del Chiablese, son of Carlo Emanuele III and Elisabetta di Lorena, resided (hence the building's name). It is also where the first Queen of Italy, Regina Margherita, was born. Until 1995 it housed the city's cinema collection and is now home to the *Sorprintendenza per I Beni Ambientali e Architettonici e Archeologici*, a state cultural institute charged with the upkeep of Turin's architectural, environmental and archaeological treasures.

★ Duomo di San Giovanni Battista

piazza San Giovanni, **T** 011 4361540. *0800-1200, 1500-1900.*
Map 2, B6, p252

The façade of Turin's cathedral to her patron saint, St John the Baptist, is the only remnant of Renaissance architecture in the city. The cathedral was built between 1491-98 by order of Cardinal Domenico della Rovere on the site of three 14th- century basilicas.

The making good of oaths is something of a theme among Turin's churches as the Superga basilica had similar origins to the Chiesa di San Lorenzo

The cathedral was designed by the Tuscan architect, Meo del Caprino, and has a classical white marble façade crowned with a typanum and three portals with carved reliefs also by Caprino. The fine wooden doors were carved in 1714-15 by Carlo Maria Ugliengo. The cathedral's 60 m Romanesque bell tower soars above the campanile di Sant'Andrea, originally built in 1468 and re-erected by Juvarra in 1720, and Guarini's famous octagonal cupola to the **Cappella della Santa Sindone** (see below). It is a symbol of the city which, until a fire in 1997, housed the city's most famed asset, the other thing most people associate with Turin beyond Fiat and the superstar footballers of Juventus: the famous Shroud. The cathedral is laid out on a Latin cross plan with three aisles flanked by decorative side chapels featuring frescoes, statues, polyptychs and paintings by masters of the Piemontese school from the 15th to the 17th centuries. A copy of the Shroud is on display on the left by the entrance and the cathedral isn't as full of tourists as you might expect. It is pretty authentic to the lay eye and, consequently if a little cynically, rather dull: it is, after all, just a very old piece of linen with some quite indistinct markings on it.

★ Cappella della Santa Sindone
Currently closed for restoration. Map 2, B6, p252

Accessed via the two black marble staircases on either side of the cathedral's presbytery the Cappella della Santa Sindone was from 1694-1997 home of the much-debated Turin Shroud. The chapel, with its famous cupola, is the work of the Modenese abbot-architect Guarino Guarini, commissioned by Carlo Emanuele II, who wanted to build a suitable resting place for the Shroud for its arrival from Chambery in France. The chapel is round and furnished with marble of different shades of black, white and grey, studded with bronze stars. At the centre is the altar where the silver box containing the Shroud was once located. Above, the interior of the cupola, composed of overlapping layers like a matchstick house, is designed to spiral infinitely upwards as if to heaven. In all there are 36 arches leading up to a 12-pointed star with a dove at the centre. The whole interior of the chapel is full of symbolic figures and geometric patterns hinting at the absolute harmony of the universe: the three of the Trinity, nine to symbolize the hour of Christ's death and 12, the number of the apostles. Enhanced by the play of *chiaroscuro* – light and dark– through the windows in the cupola's ceiling, white funerary monuments to the Savoy kings stand out against the dark marble. The chapel was ravished by a fire in April 1997 and many precious elements of the interior were damaged or destroyed. For this reason the chapel is still under restoration and therefore inaccessible to the public. Miraculously, and adding to its own mythology, the Holy Shroud was saved by its silver box and retrieved intact by Turin's firemen. The Shroud is now fiercely guarded in the left-hand transept of the cathedral and only makes the most occasional of appearances, most lately during the Millennium Jubilee celebrations.

Via Roma
Map 2, G7-D6, p252-253

While not the city's most elegant or atmospheric, via Roma is Turin's most fashionable street, a glistening, arcaded Champs-Elysées of boutiques, commercial centres, banks, cinemas and bars. The top half of the road, down to piazza San Carlo, was the main artery of Turin's early 17th-century urban expansion when it was called the *contrada nuova*. Although outwardly original and baroque in style, this section was actually rebuilt as such in 1931. The southern half of via Roma, designed by Marcello Piacentini and built between 1933-37, is visibly more modern and resonant of the fascist architecture of the Mussolini era.

Piazzetta CLN

Map 2, F6, p252

Between piazza San Carlo and piazza Carlo Felice is this small piazzetta to the *Comitato di Liberazione Nazionale*, built in 1933. There are two decorative fountains behind the twin churches, adorned with statues depicting the rivers Po and the Dora. In via Teofilo Rossi nearby, is the imposing 17th- century Palazzo Bricherasio, home to the **Fondazione Palazzo Bricherasio**, **T** 011 5711811, www.palazzobricherasio.it, *Mon 1430-1930, Tue, Wed, Sun 0930-1930, Sat 0930-2230, € 6.20, guided visits on request*, which hosts high-profile contemporary art exhibitions. It was also famously the place where the deed of the first Fiat factory was signed in 1898.

Piazza San Carlo

Map 2, E6 , p252

Without doubt the most beautiful of all Turin's piazzas, San Carlo stands at the mid-point of via Roma, a focus of retail, cultural and café life. Superbly harmonious and symmetrical, the rectangular square, with the elegant porticoed yellow and white façades of baroque noble houses, was designed by Carlo di Castellamonte to be the salon of the city's intellectual life and was completed in 1638. At the centre stands the fine bronze equestrian monument (known as *il Caval de Brons* – the bronze horseman) to Emanuele Filiberto, putting away his sword after the victorious battle of San Quintino, an 1838 work by Carlo Marochetti. On the southern end of the piazza stand the churches of **San Carlo**, **T** *011 5620922, 0800-1200, 1500-1900*, dedicated to Saint Charles Boromeo by

> ! The torinese chocolate *Giandujotto* takes its name
> • from the carnival character Gianduja, a cheerful and
> good-humoured symbol of the Piedmont region.

Carlo Emanuele I, and **Santa Cristina**, **T** 011539281, *0800-1200, 1500-1900*, both from 17th century, the latter designed Carlo di Castellamonte with a façade by Filippo Juvarra. At number 183 is the **Palazzo Isnardi di Caraglio**, home to the city's Accademia Filarmonica since 1839. Partially rebuilt by Benedetto Alfieri, this palazzo (only open for temporary exhibitions) contains magnificent 18th-century-style rooms. Piazza San Carlo was always the hub of Turin's café society and underneath its porticos are some of the city's most historic cafés still with their original furnishings. At night the piazza pulses with life, as the local well-dressed youth pose on their vespas and in their Fiat Puntos.

Northeast – University and Borgo Po

*Northeast of piazza Castello is the heart of Turin's university life, the back streets north of via Po alive with long-haired students 'studying' in the countless bars and cafés. Rising above this is Turin's Eiffel-esque icon, **la Mole Antonelliana**, offering superb panoramic views and housing an impressive and unmissable cinema museum. The main artery east is the busy, arcaded via Po whose cobbled, antiquey feel make it one of the most enchanting streets in the city. Across the river and past the unmissable nightlife of the **Murazzi**, is **la collina torinese**, Turin's rive droite – known as la Zona Crimea – and most exclusive residential area. With the spectral church of the **Gran Madre** at its fulcrum, the view is one of undulating forested hills nested by grand 19th-century and liberty-style villas. Behind these stretch hectare after hectare of wooded parkland. Brooding and Kafkaesque by winter, this area of the city exudes the sense of a greater, observing force, making it the heart of **black magic** Turin. Far away on a distant hillside stands the **Basilica di Superga**, once Turin's saviour but now a place of romance and haunting tragedy in equal measure.*

▸▸ See Sleeping p128, Eating and drinking p146.

◉ Sights

★ La Mole Antonelliana
via Montebello 20, **T** 011 8125658. *Tue-Sun 0900-2000, Sat until 2300, Mon closed.* Map 2, C9, p253

A lone spire towering above the city, the extraordinary Mole Antonelliana is without doubt the symbol and icon of Turin visible for miles around, providing sweeping vistas over the city and north to the Alps. On the top, 167.5 m above ground, sits a three-dimensional iron star which replaced the original iron angel that fell off in a hurricane in 1904.

The tower takes its name from the architect Alessandro Antonelli who was originally charged with designing a synagogue for the city's Jewish population. Instead, what he conceived was a curious mixture of neoclassical, neogothic and pure fantasy that, but for its straight lines and symmetry, might have been designed by the Catalan genius, Antoni Gaudi. However, to compare the building to anything else would be to deny its uniqueness. The conflict between adhering to tradition and striking out for a new architectural language is palpable and in fact many consider Antonelli's creation to have been seminal in sparking a fever of new metropolitan architecture that subsequently swept over Europe culminating in the Eiffel Tower, which the Mole precedes by some 20 years. Antonelli conceived his design in 1836 and building took place from 1863 until 1869 when it was discontinued by the Jewish Community. The Mole was once the highest stone building in Europe until it had to be reinforced with iron following a tornado in 1953. There are 1,040 steps leading up to the very top but these are forbidden to the public. Instead you'll be relieved to know that since 1961 an *ascensore panoramico* (panoramic lift) has carried visitors up to the mid-way terrace at 85 m from where great views can still be enjoyed. As part of Turin's devotion to the contemporary arts, the dome carries an exhibition of lights and numbers, *Luci d'Artista,* including *Il volo dei numeri* (the flight of the numbers) by Mario Merz. For what it's worth, the Mole Antonelliana also appears on the back of the two centimes euro coin. As befits a structure of such avant-garde design, the Mole also houses Turin's Museo Nazionale del Cinema, by repute the best cinema museum in Europe and definitely worth a visit.

★ Museo Nazionale del Cinema
via Montebello 20, **T** 011 8125658, www.museonazionaledelcinema.org *Tue-Sun 0900-2000, Sat until 2300, Mon closed.* € *6.80 (includes panoramic lift). Map 2, 9, p253*

Opened in 2000, the unique internal space of the Mole Antonelliana has been converted to superb effect to house Italy's Museo Nazionale del Cinema, designed by Francois Confino. The museum is laid out on four different levels and features the ultimate in museum technology in a perfect marriage of interactivity and entertainment, alongside history, science and a matchless collection of artefacts. The collection comprises some 3,400 objects, machines and devices from the early days of cinema; over 300,000 film posters and adverts; a cinematheque of 7,200 classics and a library of over 20,000 books and documents including the original scripts and scores of films like *Psycho* and *The Godfather – Part II.* Visitors work their way up from the ground floor through the history of cinema and exhibits devoted to such as aspects as divas, costumes, special effects and animation. Don't miss the holy grail of Fellini's famous hat, coat and scarf as you continue up to the pièce de resistance inside the dome of the Mole. Here, in a nod to the tower's original conception as a synagogue, is the *Aula del Tempio,* an atrium of 10 chapels where in the luxury of cushions and chaises longues visitors can immerse themselves in projections of different genres of film from Bunuel's absurdist cinema to horror flicks. Films are shown on a loop with detailed timetables of showings. Virtually the whole gamut of cinema schools are on show: it is truly unmissable.

> ### Turin – capital of cinema

Long before Italy's famous Cinecitta studios were built outside Rome, Turin was the centre of Italian cinema. The city was the birthplace of the first Italian film production companies and was where many of Italy's early and subsequent classics were filmed, such as *Cabiria* (1914) by Giovanni Pastrone, *War and Peace* (1956) by King Vidor, *La donna della domenica* (1975) by Comencini and *Profondo Rosso* (1975) by Turin's answer to Hitchcock, Dario Argento. For over a decade Turin has hosted the *Festivale di Cinema Giovane*, now internationally acclaimed as a scouting point for new international cinema talent and an alternative to the stuffy Venice festival. And nowadays Turin is back in favour as a location among Italian producers and directors, as witnessed by recent Italian hits *Prefersico il rumore del mare* (2000) by Mimmo Calopresti and *Santa Maradona* (2002) by Marco Ponti. And for those to whom none of the above are familiar, Turin should best be remembered as the location for Michael Caine's 1969 car-chase classic, *The Italian Job*.

Via Po
Map 2, C7-D10, p253

While via Roma displays its modern boutiquey air like a fashion label, via Po is the most subtle, distinguished and atmospheric of Turin's boulevards. It is a pleasure to stroll up and down its arcades, or to delve into some of the city's oldest, most refined shops including bookdealers, chocolatiers and art galleries. The street is also a favourite of Turin's student population. Betrundled by ageing orange trams, the cobbled street slopes gently down to the banks of the river Po, at its delta opening out into the vast expanse of piazza Vittorio Veneto. At number 17, the Palazzo

Universita was the last work of the architect Michelangelo Garove in 1713 while the elegant villa of the Palazzo Accorsi at number 55 houses the **Museo delle Arti Decorative**.

Palazzo Università
via Po 17. *Main building accessed around the corner at via Verdi 6 .* *Map 2, C8, p253*

Turin's university was originally founded in 1404 and has been present permanently in the city since 1566. Its main building is a magnificent architectural statement of learning. Built between 1713-20 on designs by Michelangelo Garove, the first sight is of an impressive courtyard with a double loggia of arcades studded with imperious statues and busts. Inside the main hall are paintings by Sebastiano Ricci, Sebastiano Conca and Francesco Trevisiani taken from the Cappella di Sant'Uberto in Venaria Reale (see p101).

Museo delle Arti Decorative (Fondazione Pietro Accorsi)
via Po 55, **T** 011 8129116, www.fondazioneaccorsi.it *Tue-Sun 1000-2000, Thu until 2300, Mon closed. Guided tours only.* € *6.20 (ticket includes guide).* *Map 2, D10, p253*

Spread over 26 rooms, this museum is designed to recreate the decor of an 18th- century noble residence, albeit a rather exaggerated and lavish one. Compiled from the collection of an antique collector, Pietro Accorsi (famous apparently for handling the sale of Giorgione's *Tempesta*), every detail is observed from furniture and paintings to crystal and silverware, bronzes, porcelain, majolica and carpets.

!

● While writing *Ecce Homo* in Turin in 1888-9, German philosopher Friedrich Nietzsche is said to have embraced a horse of the Turin postal service on via Po during one of his fits of madness.

The absence of romantic frills, the faith in one's own work, the self-effacing native distrust, as well as the confident feeling of taking part in the dynamics of the vast world and not being in a closed province; the pleasure of tempering life with irony and a clear, rational intelligence.

Italo Calvino, on what attracted him to Turin

Piazza Vittorio Veneto
At the end of via Po from Piazzo Castello. Map 2, D11 p253

A superb stage set for Turin's dramatic hillside backdrop focused around the Gran Madre di Dio church, piazza Vittorio Veneto is, despite its size, the most atmospheric of Turin's grandiose main squares. Continuing the theme of the arcades from via Po all around its perimeter, it was designed in the 19th-century by Giuseppe Frizzi with the aim of linking baroque Turin with the 19th-century urban developments on the other side of the Po.

I Murazzi
At the end of via Po. Map 2, D12, p253

At the end of piazza Vittorio, on either side of the Napoleonic Ponte Vittorio Emanuele over the Po, two slip roads lead down to the water's edge. To the right is a broad, flat landing bay that in Napoleonic times was used as a port. Set back from the edge, under a sequence of arches reminiscent of those on Brighton beach, is a row of former boathouses, storehouses and workshops. Designed in 1830 by Carlo Bernardo Mosca, this wall of converted industrial spaces is known by locals as the *Murazzi*, literally meaning 'bad walls', possibly on account of the louche scene that they have been famous for hosting. It's a little ironic as this is the location of Turin's best, most experimental and avant-garde bars and clubs which keep the city at the forefront of Italy's burgeoning reggae and jazz music scene. To the left of the bridge the bay narrows and is more atmospheric still. Nothing can beat coming out of the *Doctor Sax* club at 4 am on a moody winter's morning to be confronted by the moon and the silhouette of the bridge, preceded by the rushing weir across which Michael Caine's minis charged, all illuminated by the lantern of the church on the Monte dei Capuccini.

Il ponte Vittorio Emanuele I

Map 2, D12, p253

This pretty bridge connecting piazza Vittorio to the right bank and the foot of the Chiesa della Gran Madre is a creation of Turin's brief time under Naploeonic rule. Napoleon oversaw the pulling down of Turin's old city walls on the left bank, opening up the city to the right bank and replacing the 15th-century bridge with the multi-arched bridge that now stands here. With its Parisian lamps, the bridge beautifully illuminates the river and hillside at night.

Chiesa della Gran Madre di Dio

piazza della Gran Madre di Dio 4, **T** 011 8193572. *0800-1200, 1500-1900. Map 2, D13, p253*

The Gran Madre is a beautiful example of the symmetry so prevalent in Turin, with its distinctive dome and classical columns visible from the top of via Po. The street opens out into the vast expanse of piazza Vittorio Veneto and the church sits raised like a throne across the river from it. The church is a rare piece of neoclassicism in Turin, its pediment and six classical columns recalling the Pantheon in Rome (and also the Eglise de la Madeleine in Paris). The church was in fact designed by the Rome-trained architect, Ferdinando Bonsignore, and built between 1818 and 1831. Bonsignore was commissioned to design a church fit to celebrate the return of the Savoys to the throne following the end of the Napoleonic reign and the Treaty of Paris in 1814. The church is the main focal point of the right bank nestled in the natural amphitheatre of the hills. At the foot of the steps is a monument to Vittorio Emanuele I. The steps lead up to the entrance, above which is a depiction of the Virgin being prayed to by the governors of Turin. These were the steps down which Michael Caine's three minis were chased by the *carabinieri* in *The Italian Job*, charging in a criss-cross pattern while a wedding celebration carried on obliviously.

The Gran Madre has an important place in the folklore of Turin as a pole of magical forces. The church is said to stand on a point of magical energy and some even maintain the church guards the Holy Grail in its foundations.

Black magic sights
Map 2, p252

Magical energy and mysterious fog envelopes Turin to the extent that many see it as a seat of powerful supernatural forces, and there are many places to seek out this special atmosphere. The **Holy Grail** is said to lie in the foundations of the Gran Madre church (above) and some of the statues in front of the church have been linked with the prophecies of Nostradamus, who lived in Turin for several years. **Piazza Solferino**, the **Fontana Angelica**, Giovanni Riva's 1928 creation which represents the four seasons, is supposed to be the gateway to the Universe. The **parco Tesoriera**, known to believers as 'the devil's park' in Corso Francia, is supposedly the place to go at night for a rare sighting of a famous ghost on horseback.

The area around **piazza Castello**, on the other hand, is deemed to be the 'white heart' of the city and the centre of its positive energy. In the church of **Corpus Domini** (in the piazzetta of the same name) is a grail that was the subject of a miracle: it supposedly flew free of a climbing thief's swagbag and stayed airborn, only coming down to earth again when the bishop prayed it to do so. Then of course there is the Shroud and also a cross made from the same wood as Christ's cross, said to lie under the **Basilica di Maria Ausiliatrice**. There are also said to be **Grotte Alchimiche** under Palazzo Madama – caves where the Savoys kept alchemists in an attempt to make gold. The most magical point in the city is said to be the gateway through to the **Palazzo Reale** between the two equestrian statues of Castor and Pollux. The invisible line which joins them is said to divide the diabolic and the holy.

▶ Black magic city

You don't have to believe in black magic to feel the sense of mystery that pervades much of Turin, especially down by the weir on the Po on a foggy winter's night. It might be enough to assign this to some of the strange and powerful monuments and sights that are unique to the city: the bizarre form of the Mole Antonelliana; the cavernous tombs of the Egyptian museum, unexpected in such a famously industrial city; the memorial to the dead Torino footballers on the ill-fated Superga hill; or the presence of the much-debated and compelling Turin Shroud. Turin is, in actual fact, known worldwide to be a pole of both black and white magic; a point on a triangle of white, good magic with Lyon and Prague, and a point on a (slightly odd-shaped) triangle of black magic with London and San Francisco.

There are many reasons for this: firstly the predominance of symbolic buildings, sculptures and symbols such as rosaries,

dragon, masks, dogs and lions in the city; secondly because it is at the confluence of the Po and the Dora rivers which are said to represent the sun and the moon and at whose meeting point druids used to meet in the approach to the summer solstice. Turin is also allegedly a nexus of energy channels which envelop the planet, the existence of which was first mooted by the ancient Chinese. There is a legend about the creation of the city placing its beginning in 15th century BC with the ancient Egyptians, led by Prince Eridano who named the river Po. As with all ancient Roman settlements, there were four gates representing the four cardinal points and the main Roman road followed the rising sun.

Despite the above, don't go thinking that the average Torinesi is into snakes, voodoo and weird urban rituals. Most locals prefer to love the fog and brooding atmosphere of their home town.

Piazza Statuto and the area around and along Corso Francia is said to be the 'black heart' of the city. This is because it is in the west and therefore satanic, as the west is where the sun sets and sunset marks the threshold betweeen good and evil. There used to be a cemetery under the piazza, stretching out in a fan under the connecting streets. The cemetery was called *vallis occisorum*, hence the modern name of the quarter, Valdocco. Coincidentally, the centre of the piazza happens to be entrance to the operations room of Turin's sewers, the same place where legend places the gateway to hell. The neighbouring streets of **via Barabaroux** and **via Bonelli** are also supposed to be charged with evil spirits, particularly emanating from the churches, **la Chiesa della Misericordia** and **la Chiesa di Santa Maria**.

Depending on your inclination, all of this may seem entirely plausible or simply wishful sorcery. However, there is no denying the city's atmosphere of mystery and extraordinary concentration of mystical objects. Gustavo Rol was the great champion of his home town's spirituality and his and many other books on the subject can be found in the Libreria Esoterica Arethusa at via Po 2.

Chiesa di Santa Maria del Monte
via Giardino 35, **T** 011 6604414. *Daily, 0800-1200, 1500-1900.*
Map 2, F13, p253

The Monte dei Cappuccini, a wooded hilltop rising up to the right of the Gran Madre church, is a favourite among Torinesi for Sunday strolls. Atop the hill, illuminated atmospherically at night, is the church of Santa Maria del Monte. The church was commissioned in 1584 for the local community of Capuccin monks and designed by Ascanio Vitozzi. However, the church took many years to finish and was not finally consecrated until 1656. The building was overseen first by Vitozzi and then by Amedeo di Castellamonte and thus is a slight cocktail of styles. The principal feature is the lovely octagonal dome by Vitozzi, beautiful from both inside and out. The church was recently decorated with small blue lights called *Piccoli Spiriti Blu* (little blue spirits) by Rebecca Horn as part of an exhibit in the annual *Luci d'Artisti* contemporary arts festival. The exhibit was such a success that it may become a permanent feature.

Museo Nazionale della Montagna
via G Giardino 39, **T** 011 6604104, www.museomontagna.org
Daily 0900-1900 . € 5. *Map 2, F13, p253*

Just over an hour from the Alps is the appropriate location for Italy's national mountaineering museum, next to the Chiesa di Santa Maria del Monte. The museum is dedicated to Luigi di Savoia, Duke of the Abruzzi, one of the great 19th-century characters of Italy's mountaineering history. The duke was reputedly more interested in his expeditions than matters of court and managed the feat, far more significant in those days, of climbing 7,500 m up K2. The museum has various objects and documents on alpinism that are of fairly niche interest to all but enthusiasts of the mountain. It is also the headquarters of Italy's premier mountaineering club.

Villa Abegg
Closed to the public. A section of the gardens are open on Sat and Sun, May-Sep 0900-1900, Oct-Apr 0900-1700. *Map 1, G7, p251*

The Villa Abegg is one of the great grandiose villa residences of Turin's exclusive hillside. The building was erected by order of the Madama Reale, the French wife of Vittorio Amedeo I and built between 1648-53. It is said that in the solitude of this country residence the queen indulged her affair with Filippo, duke of the nearby town of Aglie. When Turin was under Napoleonic rule, the Villa Abegg is also supposed to have been the favoured residence of Paolina Bonaparte. Impressive, atmospheric and shrouded by dense gardens, the Villa Abegg was a major protagonist in the 1975 thriller film *Profondo Rosso* by Dario Argento.

Villa della Regina

strada di Santa Margherita 40. *Currently closed for restoration, due to reopen as a museum and exhibition space.*
Map 1, E8, p250

The most magnificent of the grand residences on Turin's right bank, the Villa della Regina has recently been added to UNESCO's list of world heritage sites. The double loggia, curved entrance steps and terrace decorated with statues display an almost Palladian symmetry and sense of proportion. It was the design of Ascanio Vitozzi, conceived in 1618 and built between 1620-57. The villa was built at the behest of Cardinal Maurizio di Savoia who founded his *Accademia dei Solinghi* here, a circle of philosophical and mathematical discussion and at the time a significant hotbed of anti-French thinking. The villa was subsequently the favourite demeure of Anna Maria d'Orleans and Maria Antonia Borbone. The interior features a salon with frescos by Daniel Seyter and Corrado Giaquinto (Crosato).

★ Basilica di Superga

strada Basilica di Superga 73, **T** 011 8997456. € *3 dome,* € *3 tombs,* € *5 combined entry. 0900-1200, 1500-1830. Map 1, A8, p250*

The spectral yellow form of the Superga basilica stands on a distant hill of the same name, surveying Turin like a guardian angel. Indeed, the church began its life as a protrectress: the story goes that in 1706, King Vittorio Amedeo II climbed the hill to survey the positions of the invading Franco-Spanish army. He prayed to the Virgin and swore that if she would protect the city of Turin he would build a votive church to her there in recognition of her divine intervention. A few days later, on 7 September, the Piemontese defeated the French and Spanish in the Battle of Turin and after the treasury had recovered from the drain of the war work began on making good Vittorio Amedeo's oath. The work took 15 years. From Sassi, at the foot of the hill, you can reach the basilica either by car or by using the quaint mountain railway with its 1930s wooden carriages and original station architecture. Trains depart hourly on the hour, *0900-1200, 1400-2000, Sat 0900-2000*.

The king commissioned his favourite architect, Filippo Juvarra, to design the church to represent a continuation of the flattened hillside to a summit. It is an impressive, slightly haunting hulk of a building with a grandiose baroque entrance acting as a façade to a long and externally simple main body. The entrance itself has eight magnificent Corinthian columns raised above a set of steps above which rises a double-tiered cupola flanked by two symmetrical belltowers. Inside is a large cloister and the chapel with the statue of the Madonna to which Vittorio Amedeo II supposedly prayed. However, the main attraction of the site is the vast mausoleum in the crypt (*entry € 3*). It is dedicated to the Savoy Dynasty with the tombs of dukes and kings from Vittorio Amedeo II to Carlo Alberto, designed by Juvarra's nephew, Francisco Martinez. Next to the cloister there is the famous *Sala dei Papi*, a gallery of portraits of all 240 pontiffs up to the current Pope John Paul II.

Completing the rather spooky atmosphere that pervades the Superga is the **Museo del Grande Torino**, the museum to Turin's less famous football club, Torino (or *granata* as they are colloquially known, the word for the purple of their strip), accessed through the cloister (*€ 2*). In the rear garden of the building there is a shrine to the Italian equivalent of the Munich Air disaster, when on 4 May 1949 the victorious Torino team of Valentino Mazzola crashed into the hill in thick fog on their way back from a successful European campaign. There were no survivors from Italy's finest team of the moment, eight of whom were Italian internationals. By night looking down on Turin, the city shimmers as if hovering, waiting to take off and disappear. By day from its altitude of 670 m the best views available reach as far as the Alps, the Matterhorn and Mont Blanc.

Turin's shrine

Guardian angel and graveyard of footballers, the Superga is a local pilgrimage site

Parco della Rimembranza, parco Europa and parco Leopardi

strade della Valsalice. *Winter 0900-1700, summer 0800-2200.* *Map 1, E8, , I8, G7, p250-251*

There are a succession of beautiful wooded parks in the hills above Turin. Less than 10 km and a 10 to 15-minute drive southeast from the centre is the **parco della Rimembranze**, dedicated to Italy's dead from the First World War, occupying the whole of the Colla della Maddelena hill. On the peak of the hill, at 715 m above sea level, is the *Faro della Vittoria*, a triumphal statue from 1928 by Edoardo Rubino. Further on is the **parco Europa**, also known as **parco Cavoretto**, one of the most beautiful areas of the Turin hillside with a bar, restaurants and a maze of paths in the woods. It is perfect for relaxing and a break from the boulevards of the city. Lower down by the river, **parco Leopardi** is soothing and pretty.

Southeast

*Amid elegant narrow streets and landscaped piazzettas, majestic baroque palazzi house the city's finest museums: the **Galleria Sabauda**, a priceless collection of paintings from the 14th to the 17th centuries, and the **Museo Egizio**, the largest collection of Egyptian art and artefacts outside Cairo. Nearby, the Savoys made their country pleasuredome on the banks of the river Po in the tranquil **parco Valentino**. And so from one aristocracy to another, we go south from the Savoys to the Agnellis, the dynasty that shaped Turin as a powerhouse of industrial design. A hundred years on, the Renzo Piano-restored **Lingotto complex**, the **Mirafiori plant** and the **Palazzo Vela** are monuments to the age of Futurism and Post-Modernism. Many of the famous designs that have burned up and down* autostradas *worldwide for decades emerged from these workshops, as the **Museo Dell' Automobile** testifies.*

⯈ *See Sleeping p125, Eating and drinking p149.*

◉ Sights

★ Galleria Sabauda

via Accademia delle Scienze 6, **T** 011 547440, *Tue-Sat, 0830-1930 (until 2330 on public holidays that fall on Saturdays), € 4.13, € 8 for a visit combined with the Museo Egizio. Map 2, D7, p253*

In the great tradition of monarchs, the dukes and duchesses of the House of Savoy (in Italian, *la casa sabauda*) were great collectors and patrons of the arts. The Galleria Sabauda exhibits the royal collections from Carlo Emmanuele I (1532-1630) to Carlo Alberto (1798-1849). The enormous collection features works by the Piemontese masters who worked at the Savoy court, as well as other Italian masters and many Flemish and Dutch masters. This makes the Galleria Sabauda one of the most important art galleries in Italy.

The museum is divided into seven sections over two floors of the Palazzo dell'Accademia delle Scienze which shares the space with the Museo Egizio. The first section is devoted to the Piemontese school from the 14th to the 16th centuries including a dramatic *Crocifissione* by one of Piedmont's foremost artists of the period, Gaudenzio Ferrari (1475-1546). The next section deals with various Italian schools between the 14th and the 16th centuries including works by Beato Angelico, il Pollaiolo and il Bronzino. The third section on this floor is devoted to the Flemish and Dutch collection by Principe Eugenio di Savoia Soissons. Among many still-life and landscape canvasses, the most notable works are *Le Stigamate di San Francesco* by Jan Van Eyck, *La Passione di Cristo* by Hans Memling and *Portrait of an Old Man* by Rembrandt. On the floor above, the exhibition continues with the collection of Emanuele Filiberto and Carlo Emanuele I from 1550-1630. Included in this are works by il Guercino, il Bassano, the *Cena in Casa di Simone* by Veronese, *L'Annunziazione* by Gentileschi and *la Dejanira tentata dalla furia* by Rubens. Masterpieces such as Francisco Cairo's anguished *Erodiade*

Turin

Capital of baroque

Turin is sometimes referred to as a capital of the baroque and has its own particular dialect of the baroque style. Turin's baroque architecture is not the twirly vainglorious Papal marble of Bernini and Maderna's Rome; it is instead a more sobre, regal and, at times, austere version where the movement and fantasy in the design is always tempered by a sense of pragmatism, function and a desire to leave the humble prime materials, such as the red brick, bare to speak for themselves. Turin's baroque years lasted from the late 16th century to the mid-18th century, masterminded by the great architectural dynasties of the Alfieri and Castellamonte families together with Guarino Guarini, Michelangelo Garove and Filippo Juvarra. They started with the expulsion of the French in 1562 when the city became the capital of the Savoy Dukedom. The Savoy Dukes were great patrons of the arts and, like any overlord,

sought to leave an imprint of their reign through the architecture of the day. Carlo Emanuele I oversaw the redevelopment of Turin's medieval proportions around piazza Castello and down the axis of via Roma. This was followed with the second expansion south and eastwards according to Amedeo di Castellamonte's 1673 plan. In 1714 Turin began to push west under the influence of Filippo Juvarra. Turin's piazzas are the real shop-windows of the city's baroque dialect but the unique style pervades all aspects of its architecture from important state buildings such as Palazzo Carignano and Accademia delle Scienze and private residences such as Palazzo Barolo and Palazzo Saluzzo Paesana to the more obvious examples of the royal buildings of piazza Castello and the churches of Santa Cristina, Santa Croce and San Filippo Neri, and most spectacularly, the Cappella della Sacra Sindone.

con la testa del Battista and an oil by Van Dyck, *I figli di Carlo I d'Inghilterra*, a beautiful and emotive depiction of Charles' I children, are also on display. There then follow some lovely depictions of Turin through the ages before the exhibition concludes with *Venere e Marte con Cupido* by Veronese and one of the oldest works in the museum, Duccio's *Madonna in trono con Bambino e due angeli*.

★ Museo Egizio

via Accademia delle Scienze 6, **T** 011 561 7776,
www.museoegizio.org *Daily except Mon 0830-1930. € 6.20 , € 3.10 for EU citizens aged 18-25, € 8 combined entry with Galleria Sabauda. Guided tours every Sat. Free to holders of Torino Card. Map 2, D7, p253*

Turin is home to the the largest and most important collection of ancient Egyptian art and artefacts outside Cairo itself, which comes as a surprise to many. It's one of Turin's many hidden charms and all goes back to a small royal collection which has grown over the centuries. In 1630 the Savoy royal family moved house from Chambery and transferred the Mensa Isiaca and their three large Egyptian statues to Turin. The collection began to grow to its current size under the reign of Carlo Felice and it was moved in 1824 to its current residence in the Palazzo dell'Accademia della Scienze. Following fashion and revived interest in Egyptiana, sparked by Napoleon's expeditions and discoveries, Carlo Felice decided to buy the Drovetti colletion consisting of over 8,000 pieces. The cataloguing and installation of these pieces as well as the gradual tripling of the collection was due to the archaeologist Ernesto Schiaparelli, curator of the musem from 1894. He was responsible for the discovery and explanation of many of the important pieces from the early Egyptian civilization on display which subsequently illuminated the whole field of Egyptology.

Arranged across three floors including the basement, the exhibition passes from circa 4000 BC to around AD 400 and in the first hall there are some very important exhibits. One of the most intact and oldest examples of mummification is beautifully preserved in glass displays complete with burial gifts; the *Papiro dei Re* (the charter of kings) is also on display, the only known ancient Egyptian to list the Egyptian pharaohs in order of succession. Further on, the museum displays a mouthwatering and awe-inspiring collection of sphinxes, busts, masks and statues including those of Ramses II. On the first floor is an eerie sequence of tombs and chapels, most stunningly that of Kha and Mirit, complete with wall-paintings, more coffins and symbolic artefacts.

You could quite imagine yourself as Tintin in the *Cigars of the Pharaoh* or Rachel Weisz in *The Mummy* with all these treasures around you. Like dinosaurs, ancient Egypt continues to fascinate and Turin's museum is the second best place in the world to catch the bug. Allow yourself at least a couple of hours to explore.

Pinacoteca dell'Accademia Albertina
via Accademia Albertina 6, **T** 011 8177862, www.accademiaalbertina.torino.it *Tue-Sun 0900-1300, 1500-1900 € 4. Map 2, D9, p253*

Although Turin's state art gallery is upstaged by the Galleria Sabauda, its 300 pictures still represent an important collection of paintings, sculptures and drawings from the 15th to the 19th centuries. Spread across 12 rooms, a few highlights of the exhibition are landscapes by Christian Wehrlin, Francesco Antonio Mayerle and Daniel Seyter, *Cain and Abel* by Giulio Cesare Procaccini, still-life canvasses by Nicasius Bernaerts, depictions of the fathers of the church by Filippo Lippi and *Deposition* by Maarten van Heemskerck. The pride of the museum is the unrivalled collection of 60 cartoons of ecclesiastical iconography by Gaudenzio Ferrari, donated in 1832. The accademia also has a library containing many rare and valuable tomes and prints.

Chiesa di San Filippo Neri

via Maria Vittoria 5, **T** 011 538456. *0800-1200, 1500-1900. At the crossroads of via Maria Vittoria and via Accademia delle Scienze.*
Map 2, E7, p253

This majestic church with an imperial neoclassical façade and a four-columned Corinthian portico, was built between 1675 and 1772, undergoing the influence of many architects: Guarino Guarini, Michelangelo Garove and finally Filippo Juvarra. It has the largest church interior in Turin, a majestic single aisle flanked by stunning elliptical windows and stucco work. The church contains many art treasures, notably the main altar and paintings by Carlo Maratta, Francesco Solimena and Francesco Trevisani. Next door is the Oratorio di San Filippo, also by Juvarra, dating from 1723 and with a pretty frescoed vault, more stucco and paintings by Mattia Franceschini and both Giovanni and Sebastiano Conca.

Teatro Carignano

piazza Carignano, corner via Maria Vittoria 5, **T** 011 541136.
Map 2, E7, p253

Built originally in 1752 on a design by Benedetto Alfieri, this theatre has burnt down twice. The current building, restored in the 19th century, was completed in 1787 to designs by Giovanni Battista Feroggio. The plush theatre interior is beautifully set off by a frescoed ceiling, the work of Francesco Gonin, who also painted the ceiling in the famous *Ristorante del Cambio* next door.

Palazzo Carignano

via Accademia delle Scienze 5, **T** 011 5621147. *Map 2, D7, p253*

With its curvy alternately concave and convex façade, the red-brick Palazzo Carignano is one of Turin's most unusual baroque buildings. Designed by Guarino Guarini and built between 1679-94, the building was doubled in size in the 19th century beyond the internal courtyard with a whole wing added by Giuseppe Bollati on plans by Gaetano Ferri. Inside, two curved staircases lead up to the *piano nobile* and the elliptical ballroom which was converted into the seat of the first Subalpine Parliament in 1848 as a precursor to the birth of the Italian state in 1861. Appropriately, the palace now houses the **Museo del Risorgimento Italiano**. To the rear the comparatively blunt façade looks out onto **piazza Carlo Alberto** with a central equestrian statue to Carlo and beyond the former stables of the Principe di Carignano which between 1959-73 were merged with the **Biblioteca Nazionale**.

Museo Nazionale del Risorgimento Italiano
via Accademia delle Scienze 5, **T** 011 5621147, www.regione.piemonte.it/cultura/risorgimento *Tue-Sun 0900-1900. € 5, free to holders of Torino Card. Map 2, D7, p253*

Housed in the suitably grandiose Palazzo Carignano, the Museo Nazionale del Risorgimento Italiano is unbelievably the only museum in the country devoted to celebrating and remembering Italy's birth as a nation. After a peripatetic beginning, the museum finally opened here in 1965. The museum takes as its start point the 1706 victory of the Savoy over the invading Franco-Spanish armies, passing through the Napoleonic occupation to the first traces of an independence movement that followed the French Emperor's unseating. It also documents the formation of the statute of nationhood, the *Statuto Albertino*, the declaration of independent Italy in 1861 and the founding of the Italian parliament. In terms of exhibits, the museum features many paintings of important battles and triumphal moments such as the battles of Goito and San Martino, portraits and busts of the main protagonists such as d'Azeglio, Cavour, Mazzini and Garibaldi and documents of early

Il Risorgimento

Considering the foundation of the Roman Empire, the fact that Italy as a nation is still not even 150 years old still comes as a surprise. The brainchild of Camillo Benso di Cavour who first mooted the idea of an Italian constitution, the idea arose from the mouth of Napoleon and gained power and support through the post-Napoleonic alliances with Austria, with statesmen such as d'Azeglio and Giuseppe Mazzini as the main protagonists along with Cavour. In 1861 a united Italy was declared with Vittorio Emanuele II at its helm. Having already had one rebirth in the renaissance, this moment was called *il risorgimento*, meaning more specifically 'resurrection'. Visitors to Italy will know that it betrays its youth through the strong identity and rivalry between its constituent regions, be they Piedmont, Tuscany or Campania, and in culinary, linguistic and artistic rivalry. Even greater is the love-hate relationship between the North and the South.

nationalist propaganda. It also displays the texts of the statutes and recreations of the prison cell of the revolutionary writer Silvi Pellico and the Parliament chamber that was never used because power was transferred to Florence in 1865. From an objective point of view, the museum is a fascinating and compelling account of the birth of a nation whose youth still surprises.

Piazza Carlina
Via Accademia Albertina Map 2, E9, p253

This area of Turin is notable for its many interlinking little piazzas. Also known as piazza Carlo Emanuele II, this square was once the site of Turin's wine market. At the centre of the piazza is a monument to Camillo Benso di Cavour, one of the founders of the

Italian constitution. Surrounding the square are a number of notable buildings: at number 13, the Palazzo Roero di Guarene with a baroque façade from 1730 by Filippo Juvarra; at number 4, the Collegio delle Province, the work of Bernardo Vittone; on the southern side the church of **Santa Croce**, **T** 011 8126703, *0800-1200, 1500-1900*, also designed by Juvarra.

Next door to piazza Carlina is **piazza Cavour**, built in 1835 on the site of a former city fortification. Further on still is **piazza Maria Teresa**, encircled by many elegant palazzi including at via Giolitti 46 the Casa Ponzio Vaglia by Alessandro Antonelli (of the Mole Antonelliana).

Museo Regionale della Scienze Naturali
via Giolitti 36, **T** 011 4323080. *Wed-Mon 1000-1900. € 5.*
Map 2, E10, p253

The imposing and rather forbidding mass of this former hospital was designed by Amedeo di Castellamonte in 1680. The hospital is now the seat of Turin's natural science museum, the **Museo Regionale delle Scienze Naturali**, founded in 1978 and consisting in a relatively unspectacular collection of geological, zoological, botanical and mineral exhibits.

Stazione Porta Nuova
C.so Vittorio Emanuele II *Map 2, H7, p253*

Turin's impressive railway terminus is equal in stature, industrial grandeur and atmosphere to Milan's Centrale station. The station was built between 1863-68 on the site of the former city fortifications and replaced an old *imbarcadero* used solely for trains to Genoa. The design of the station was a collaboration between the architects Alessandro Mazzucchetti and Carlo Ceppi. Built just after the *Risorgimento*, its unusual, ornate façade with white and blushed stone, delicate ironwork and windows above towering

majestic columns constitutes a very emphatic statement of
national pride. The fortunes of Porta Nuova are shortly to change
as Porta Susa becomes Turin's principal rail link and Eurostar hub.

Ponte Umberto I
Map 2, G12, p253

Turin's most majestic bridge over the river Po is at the end of the
imperial main boulevard of Corso Vittorio Emanuele II. A triple-arch
and ornate construction, it was designed by Vincenzo Micheli and
Enrico Ristori and built between 1903-07 on the ruins of the
19th-century Ponte di Maria Teresa. Along both sides of the bridge
are allegorical bronze statues by Luigi Contratti and Cesare Reduzzi.
At the entrance to the parco Valentino on the city side of the bridge
is the Arco Monumentale all'Artigliere, a monumental arch.

★ Parco del Valentino
C.so Massimo d'Azeglio. *Winter 0900-1700, summer 0800-2200.*
Map 2, H10-11, p253

Stretching for 30 soothing riverside hectares between the two
bridges across the Po is Turin's most suggestive, atmospheric and
romantic park. It is a perfect place for gentle Sunday strolls and
lovers' trysts. Parco del Valentino owes its current appearance to the
design of the 19th- century French landscape architect, Jean-Pierre
Barillet-Deschamps. He designed the park's system of paths, woods,
artificial mounds and little valleys, and its lake and horse riding
grounds in 1864. The park was opened as Italy's first public garden in
1856, a few years before this. The *Valentino*, as the locals refer to it,
contains a number of Turin's most interesting and important cultural
sites including the **Castello Valentino** and its **Orto Botanico**
(botanical garden), the **Borgo Medioevale** model medieval castle
and village, and the exhibition complex of **Torino Esposizioni**.
Turin hosted many international fairs from 1884 onwards. The 1961

expo gave birth to the **Giardino Roccioso** (rock garden) at the park's centre by Giuseppe Rati, a kaleidoscope of flowers watered and interspersed by terraces of rock arrangements, fountains and streams. The beautiful rose garden, **Il Roseto**, was added in 1965. The park also has many notable and pretty fountains and statues such as the **Fontana dei Dodici Mesi** at its southern end, designed by Carlo Ceppi in 1898 for the 50th anniversary of the Statuto Albertino.

Castello Valentino
parco del Valentino. *Map 2, H11, p253*

By far the most famous and majestic building in the Parco Valentino is the former royal castle. Its horseshoe-shaped courtyard resembles a cross between the Louvre and a chateau on the Loire. But despite the unmistakable Louis XIV resonances in its grey triangular rooftops and mansard windows, the complete excess of baroque detail on its honey-coloured walls could only be Italian. It was once merely a humble boathouse until in 1564 it was bought by Duke Emmanuele Filiberto. It was then passed down the Savoy line to Carlo Emmanuele I who gave it as a present to Maria Cristina, daughter of the King of France. She made it her residence and court and from her the French influence on the architecture can be traced. She commissioned its transformation between 1630 and 1660 and the palace that grew up was the centre of the Savoy court and the core of political life in the 17th century. It was also the scene of accords, armistices and alliances formed, signed and agreed, as well as numerous opulent parties and receptions. Facing the river Po, Maria Cristina had pavilions, courtyards and porticoed galleries and terraces added to either side, while the river, hillside and dense woodland in the park added a countryside air. Maria Cristina died in 1663 and thus begun the Castello's decline and fall. Since 1906, this magnificent building has been the architecture faculty of Turin's polytechnic, an inspiring ivory tower for any student. The **Salone**

Centrale and **Stanza della Caccia** rooms still conserve and convey some of the castle's former role and splendour.

L'Orto Botanico
viale Mattioli 25, **T** 011 6612447. *Sat, Sun and public holidays 0900-1300, 1500-1900, Mon-Fri by appointment only. Closed Oct-Mar.* € *3. Map 3, A11, p255.*

Flanking the northern side of the courtyard of the Castello Valentino is Turin's botanical garden. It was founded in 1729 on the wish of Vittorio Amedeo III with the express aim of cultivating the plants that formed the basis of early 18th-century medicine. The atrium was added in 1894 and in its entirety the complex is considered one of the most important Italian centres of botanical studies. It follows on from a pedigree which, botany enthusiasts will be interested to know, saw such herbal luminaries as Allioni, Balbis, Moris and Delponte work here in the 18th and 19th centuries. Second only to that in Florence, the herb garden here conserves examples of 700,000 herbs, while the pride of the gardens is the 64-volume *Iconographia Tauriensis* containing over 7,500 scientific and beautifully intricate watercolours of the plants grown here between 1800 and 1864.

Il Borgo e Rocca Medioevale
viale Virgilio, parco del Valentino, **T** 011 4431701. *Borgo: Mon-Sun 0900-1900.* € *2.58. Map 3, E12, p255*

Although appearing remarkably realistic, the *Rocca* (medieval citadel) and village at the Po riverside to the south of the park is in fact a model and therefore kind of al fresco museum. Complete with drawbridge, cobbled streets, little houses and workshops the model is an exact facsimile of medieval Piemontese architecture in 15th century. It was conceived and built for the 1884 Expo by Giuseppe Giocosa and Alfredo d'Andrade.

▶ A beautiful car is like a beautiful woman...

Some of the best, most romantic and most famous car shapes in the world started life on a Turin drawing board. The city is home to three of the great Italian dynasties of car design: Bertone, Pininfarina and Giugiaro.

Giovanni Bertone first opened his 'carradore' chassis repair shop in 1912 and was soon responsible for models such as the Fiat 527 Ardita 2500, a revolution in car design at the time; the best-selling 1954 Alfa Giulietta Sprint, the Ferrari GT 250 and Maserati 5000 GT in the 1960s, and the 1965 Fiat spider 850. In 1970 he conceived the Lancia Stratos and then went on to design for Volvo, Citroen and Opel before returning with the ubiquitous Fiat Punto in the 1990s.

Giugiaro, an employee of Bertone's son, produced the Maserati Ghibli and De Tommaso Mangusta before such staples as the Alfasud, the Fiat Uno and the Lancia Delta and Prisma. But the real kings of Italian car design are the Pininfarina Dynasty.

Battista Farina, detto Pinin, was born in 1893 and his Cistalia Coupe, a sought-after classic today, was the first car to become an exhibit in New York's MOMA as well as winning many prestigious Gran Turismo races. The Pinifarina family became virtually exclusive designers for Ferrari with Sergio Pininfarina conceiving the Ferrari Dino 246 T to commemorate the passing of Enzo Ferrari's son, perhaps the most beautiful car ever designed to this day.

For Sergio, "*una bella automobile è come una bella donna: possono passare gli anni ma si vede che è sempre stata bella*"
(a beautiful car is like a beautiful woman, even as the years go by you can tell she was always beautiful).

Latterly, he also designed the famous Ferrari Testarossa.

Torino Esposizioni

parco del Valentino. *Map 3, E11, p255.*

Turin has long been a host of prestigious international exhibitions and trade fairs. The modern exhibition complex of Torino Esposizioni was built in 1961 to celebrate 100 years of Italian unity and its functionalist block architecture reflects its 1960s origins. Until 1990 the complex hosted the *Salone Internazionale dell'Automobile* and it still hosts important events that keep Turin on the national cultural calendar. Around and within the complex are the **Teatro Nuovo**, the **Palazzo di Ghiaccio ice rink** and the **Palazzina Promotrice delle Belle Arti** established in 1919. The Villa Glicini building is the headquarters of Turin *Club di Scherma* (fencing club) which hosts international competitions.

Palazzo Vela (Palazzo delle Mostre)

via Ventimiglia 145. *Map 1, J7, p251*

Shaped like a sail, hence its nickname *Palazzo Vela*, this building is an iconic piece of Turin's 20th- century industrial architecture. It is part of a complex of buildings known as 'Italia 61' built to celebrate 100 years of the unification of Italy. Designed by Annibale and Giorgio Rigotti and made of reinforced concrete and glass, the building houses exhibitions, concerts and sports events. Fans of *The Italian Job* will remember the scene from the epic car chase when Michael Caine and his three gold-laden minis go up the ramp of the Palazzo Vela chased by the *carabinieri* in a rickety old police car which promptly conks out allowing the thieves to escape. Further on is the **Palazzo del Lavoro**, via Ventimiglia 201, a similarly iconic building consisting in a large square ceiling supported by metal umbrellas and 20-m concrete columns.

Best

★ Places for a great view of Turin

★ Il Lingotto
via Nizza 280. *Map 1, J6, p251*

The Lingotto building is a work of architecture every bit as important in the history of industrial modernism and the avant-garde as works of fine art from those periods. The building was born in 1923 when the newly-founded Fiat car company needed to bring its production line under one roof to maximize efficiency. When the plant was opened in the presence of King Vittorio Emanuele III, Le Corbusier called it 'a model of urbanism' and the architect of Futurism, Filippo Marinetti, called it *"la prima invenzione costruttiva futurista"* (the first constructive Futurist construction). The famous rooftop test track familiar to fans of *The Italian Job* still seems futuristic. In reality, though, delays to building caused by the First World War meant that the Lingotto plant was already behind the times and the rooftop track was impractical for speed-testing. Lingotto survived as a factory until 1982 before being superceded by the enormous Mirafiori installation. It formally closed in 1983 only for the Genoese architect, Renzo Piano, to be summoned to transform it into a multi-purpose modern Fiat showpiece. Lingotto reopened with a hotel, cinema complex, landscaped gardens, university faculty, exhibition centre and auditorium. On the top, a signature piece of Piano architecture, *la Bolla*, a spherical glass ball, acts as a conference centre complete with helipad while *Lo Scrigno*, a ship-like building, is an art gallery, **Pinacoteca Giovanni e Marella Agnelli**, *via Nizza 230, **T** 011 6862008, Tue-Sun 0900-1900, € 4*, donated to the city by Agnelli and his wife containing 25 masterpieces of painting and sculpture including works by Canaletto, Matisse, Balla and Picasso.

Fiat Mirafiori
C.so Unione Sovietica. *Map 1, K/L4, p251*

Mirafiori is the enormous factory of the Agnelli Fiat empire – Fabbrica Italiana Automobili Torino – and the hub of the industry that made Turin's fortune since the beginning of the 20th century. Designed by Vittorio Bonade Bottino and inaugurated by Mussolini on 15 May 1939, it is still Italy's largest factory and one of the largest in the world, covering over a million square metres, 300,000 of them under cover, 2.5 km-worth of test track, 7 km of tunnels and 11 km of railtrack. The Mirafiori plant attracted many Italians from the Mezzogiorno (the deep south) to seek their fortune here in the 1950s and 1960s, accounting for the rich mix of Italian dialects in Turin but also the acres of dreary working-class suburbs that characterize the south of the city.

Museo Nazionale dell'Automobile
C.so d'Italia 40, **T** 011 677666, www.museoauto.org *Tue-Sun 1000-1830, Thu until 2200.€ 5.50.   Map 1, J7, p251*

It is appropriate that the country's most important car museum should be found in the seat of the Italian capital of car production, in a country that has contributed so many great designs and so much flair to the car industry down the decades. Conceived by Amedeo Albertini, it was opened in 1960 and takes visitors on a history of the development of the car, from the evolution the tyre via early steam-powered vehicles to the present day. Cars from all over the world are represented. Among the many famous models on display is a 1901 Fiat, an Itala, winner of the 1907 Peking-Paris rally, and a Cistalia 202 as well as a Ford Model-T and, of course, a Rolls Royce Silver Ghost from 1914.

Southwest

*Marked by wide and grand tree-lined boulevards, the architecture of this area was defined by the French vogue of the 19th century spreading from Haussmann's Paris. This quarter also displays some significant testaments to Turin's defenses against French invasion of a more military sort. The underground tunnels of the **Museo Pietro Micca** retell the story of Turin's safeguard against Franco-Spanish forces thanks to the heroics of a humble miner. Located appropriately at the heart of this more modern corner of Turin is the **Galleria d'Arte Moderna (GAM)**, Turin's fine modern art collection, tracing the journey of 19th- and 20th-century art. Of all the districts of the city, this is set to be the most transformed by the 2006 Olympic revamp.*
▸▸ *See Sleeping p124, Eating and drinking p153.*

Sights

Via Pietro Micca
Map 2, E5-6, p252

In a city consisting almost entirely of horizontal and vertical gridded streets, diagonal via Pietro Micca is a bit of an anomaly. Leading southwest off piazza Castello, it is an elegant arcaded street typical of Turin's Parisian-style 19th-century elegance. Its architect Carlo Ceppi also designed the façade of the otherwise plain 16th-century Franciscan church of **San Tommaso**, **T** 011 544667, *0800-1200, 1500-1900*. Via Pietro Micca has gone down in the annals as the place where in 1894 the famous Russian ballerina and actress, Irina Lucacevich, was run over by a tram. Heading west, the street leads to the refined **piazza Solferino**. At the centre of it is Giovanni Riva's 1930 fountain symbolizing the four seasons. There is also a wonderful and moving equestrian monument to Ferdinand, Duke of Genoa, by Alfonso Balzico in 1877.

Museo Civico Pietro Micca e dell'Assedio di Torino del 1706
via Guicciardini 7a, **T** 011 546317, www.comune.torino.it/musei
Tue-Sun 0900-1900, closed Mon. € 2.58. *Map 2, E1, p252*

No words have been spared in the name of this museum to show the Torinesi's pride in the safeguard of their city by the heroic miner Pietro Micca. During the War of the Spanish Succession between 13 May and 7 September 1706, Turin was under siege to a Franco-Spanish army led by the Duke de la Feuillade. As deep as 14 m below the surface, a network of 15 km of defensive tunnels was built to try and stave off the attack. Miners were sent down into the tunnels to help repel the advances. On 28 August that year, to thwart the Franco-Spanish advances, miner Pietro Micca blew up an under-ground staircase, killing himself and fellow miners, but also many invaders, saving the city from underground attack and bringing an end to the siege. The museum houses a few remains of Turin's 16th-century fortifications and retells the heroics of Pietro Micca together with documents and reconstructions. Unearthed in 1958, about 300 m of the tunnels can still be visited on torch-lit tours.

Cittadella and Museo Storico dell'Artiglieria
corner via Cernaia and C.so Galileo Ferraris, **T** 011 5629223. *Only open for exhibitions. Free.* *Map 2, E3, p252*

Little remains of this great pentagonal 16th-century citadel commissioned by Emanuele Filiberto to celebrate the liberation of Turin in 1563. Designed by Francesco Paciotto, it once covered a much larger area. It was demolished in 1856 and all that remains now is the *mastio* (the keep), restored at the end of 19th century by Riccardo Brayda. Inside the keep is Turin's oldest museum founded in 1731, the **Museo Storico dell'Artiglieria**. The museum traces the history of artillery and firearms and includes many pieces of equipment and models from the Italian army down the centuries including machines for making gunpowder and also suitably patriotic exhibits such as flags, trophies and uniforms.

Teatro Alfieri
piazza Solferino 2, **T** 011 5623800. *Map 2, E5, p252*

Built between1855-60 on a design by Giovanni Svanascini at the behest of Zaccaria Ottolenghi, this theatre was inaugurated in 1860 to the tune of Rossini's *Moses*. Since then it has hosted a long list of divas, prima donnas, lyrical stars and poets. In 1979 it closed for a long refurbishment, finally reopening in 2002. It's a classic on the Turin theatre landscape, hosting plays by Wilde and Brecht as well as more unusual 20th-century drama from the likes of Boris Vian.

Teatro Juvarra
via Juvarra 15, **T** 011 540675. *Map 2, D2, p252*

Dedicated to Turin's most famous architect, this theatre, refurbished in 1989, is home to Turin's *Granserraglio* troupe who specialize in comic spectacles, music and dance and experimental theatre. The boards here have been graced by the likes of Lella Costa, Luciana Littiezzetto, Bruno Gambarotta and Moni Ovadia.

Chiesa di Santa Teresa
via Santa Teresa 5. *Map 2, E6, p252*

Dedicated to Santa Teresa di Avila, work began on this church in 1642 from plans by Andrea Costaguta and finished in 1764 by Filippo Juvarra who designed the beautiful façade with its double loggia of Corinthian columns. Juvarra was also responsible for many of the jewels inside, most notably the side chapels of the

Architectural gem

The Palazzo Carignano, a fine example of Turin's austere yet fluid baroque style.

Sacra Famiglia and San Giuseppe. Of particular beauty is the altar in the San Giuseppe chapel, commissioned in 1733 by Juvarra and with statues by Simone Martinez. In the Cappella di Sant'Erasmo is the mausoleum of the Madama, Maria Cristina di Francia, the queen and wife of Vittorio Amedeo I who died in 1663.

Museo della Marionetta

via Santa Teresa 5, **T** 011 5320238. *Visits by appointment only.* € 2.60. *Map 2, E5, p252*

In the rooms next door to the Teatro Gianduja, home to Turin's *Lupi* troupe of puppet artists, is the city's puppet museum. The museum itself, open during shows, has a collection of scenery, puppets, costumes, backdrops and scripts from over 200 years of performances by the *Lupi* group. Among the collection are items from around the world and a history of puppetry from around the globe.

★ Galleria d'Arte Moderna

via Magenta 31, **T** 011 5629911, www.gamtorino.it *Tue-Sun 0900-1900 (guided tours on Sun and first Fri of month).* € 5.50. *Map 2, H3, p252*

Known as GAM, Turin's outstanding contemporary art museum will quieten anyone who doubts that Turin is a city of culture. At the very avant-garde of modern art and arranged on two levels, the museums takes the visitor on a journey through artistic movements from the end of the 18th century through to the early 1990s. It covers sculpture and painting, Piemontese artists, Italian masters and numerous important works by famous international names including Balla, Modigliani, Chagall and the artists of the *Arte Povera* movement. A thorough tour of the lesser-known works and artists is highly recommended, but if you are interested in famous highlights and pressed for time you should not miss some

▶ The 2006 Winter Olympics

Turin will be the base for the 2006 Winter Olympics, although most of the events will be taking place out west in the valleys. You could say that the Olympics were a convenient means of explaining the city's regeneration but Turin has in fact been regenerating itself for a number of years. That said, the Olympic flame will certainly help to illuminate the city's treasures. The opening ceremony will be held in the refurbished Stadio Comunale, which will also host the ice hockey tournament. Next to the Stadio Comunale will be more sporting arenas for the speed-skating competition, one to be designed by the Tokyo-based architect Arata Isozaki. The area that is set to be transformed the most is the Lingotto in the southeast, where an Olympic village and number of media centres will be built on the site of the ex-Mercati Generali warehouses on via Giordano.

Torinese sentiment about the games is a little contradictory: proud of their city's turn in the limelight, they are nevertheless slightly uncomfortable that the label 'Olympic City' might obscure Turin's growing status as one of the funkiest and most modernized of Italy's cities, for which they feel it deserves attention in itself.

of the museum's most important exhibits. Among them are *Compenetrazione iridescente* (1912) by Turin's Futurist master Giacomo Balla, *La Ragazza Rosa* (1915) by Modigliani and *Bozza di Manifesto* (1920) by Ernst from the avant-garde section, and the works of Giorgio de Chirico in room 7. Room 15 has works by Klee, Picasso, Marc Chagall and Fernand Léger. Moving into the second half of the 20th century, Italy's most important recent art movement Arte Povera is well represented in rooms 20 and 21, a post-minimalist anti-commercial take on art, focusing on traditionally neglected materials like sand, earth and concrete. The abstract works of current artists such as Mario Merz, famous for his igloos, and Alighiero Boetti conclude the exhibition.

Piazza Statuto
Map 2, D1, p252

Linking via Garibaldi with the late 19th-century development of western Turin along Corso Francia, piazza Statuto was opened in 1864 with the aim to complete the symmetry of the four entrances to central Turin (alongside piazza Vittorio in the east, piazza Repubblica to the north and piazza Carlo Felice to the south). The piazza was designed by Carlo Pronis and realized by Giuseppe Bollati. At its centre is considered to be a garden *all'inglese* designed by Giuseppe Bollati and a haunting monument to the builders of the Frejus tunnel, the first of the great tunnels through the Alps, dating to 1879, as well as the point which marks Turin's latitude. Piazza Statuto is said to have inspired many of Giorgio de Chirico's metaphysical paintings.

Stadio Comunale
via Filadelfia 88. *Map 1, I5, p251*

Turin's beloved Stadio Comunale came into being as the Stadio Mussolini, designed for football and athletic competitions. Only after the war did its name change to Stadio Comunale and it became Turin's main football stadium, witnessing the growth and success of Turin's two great teams, Torino and Juventus until the Stadio delle Alpi was built for the World Cup in 1990. The stadium has also hosted concerts including Bob Marley's in 1970. The stadium is currently Juventus' training ground and there is a good chance of seeing Del Piero and friends. The stadium will soon be refurbished as it is due to host Winter Olympic events in 2006.

Stazione Porta Susa
Piazza XVIII Dicembre *Map 2, E1, p252*

Built in 1856 and therefore the older of Turin's two main railway stations, Porta Susa will soon be Turin's main station. It is set to undergo a massive, spectacular overhaul as part of Turin's 2006 Winter Olympic development. Work has already begun on architect Agostino Magnaghi's design for a large tunnel linking rail passengers with the city's new underground, taking all Turin's public transport traffic, except the trams and buses, underground.

Northwest – Roman Turin

*Turin reveals her Roman origins in the area to the northwest of piazza Castello, no better embodied than in the great Porta Palatina gate, still standing after 2,000 years. Here, narrow winding alleys still exude the secretive atmosphere of medieval times. Ignored for decades, the grid of streets north of via Garibaldi known as '**il quadrilatero**' has recently become the city's most vibrant quarter, punctuated by some of the best restaurants, bars and late lounges in the city. The area also has a collection of small intimate churches with beautiful frescoes and façades. Further north runs the river Dora and, on either side of it, the working class Balon district famous for its weekly flea market. Beyond the city's perimeter stands the **Stadio delle Alpi**, temple to that most Italian of passions, football, and in Turin more specifically, Juventus.*
▸▸ *See Sleeping p125, Eating and drinking p156.*

◉ Sights

Teatro Romano
piazzale Cesare Augusto. *Map 2, B5, p252*

Just north of the cathedral and beyond the new wing of the Palazzo Reale are the remains of the Roman town of Augusta

Taurinorum and the two main pieces of archaeological interest in the city. The Roman theatre has been dated to the first century AD, belonging therefore to the late Augustan or Tiberian period. The theatre is 120 m in diameter and the colonnaded outer ring of the gallery, some of the banks of seating and a portion of the orchestra are still visible.

Porta Palatina
via Porta Palatina. *Map 2, A5, p252*

More impressive than the remains of the theatre is the red-brick northern gate to the former Roman town, Augusta Taurinorum. It is similar to the one that forms the basis of the Palazzo Madama in piazza Castello but, standing alone, it is one of the best preserved of its kind. Like the theatre, the gate was built in the first century AD and is composed of two thick towers each with 16 sides linked by a filled-in bridge known as the *interturrium*. Linking the towers under this are two loggias of windows, one arched, the other rectangular, while underneath are four passageways, two each for carts and pedestrians. The name of the gate dates back to the Middle Ages when it was adjoined to a building, now no longer extant, called *Palatium*. Inside the gate are the remains of the courtyard with remnants of the original Roman paving. A statue of Julius Caesar stands in front.

Museo di Antichita
via XX Settembre 88c, **T** 011 5212251, *Tue-Sun 0830-1930, Mon closed.* € 4. *Map 2, A6, p252*

Fittingly for an area of the city that is of archaeological note, this museum – actually the former orangerie of the Palazzo Reale – contains a rich and valuable collection of exhibits from the prehistoric and Paleolithic periods to Greek, Roman, Etruscan and Barbarian times. The core of the collection stems from the reign of

Emanuele Filiberto but thereafter expanded significantly causing it to be moved throughout Turin. In 1723 Vittorio Amedeo II moved it from the Palazzo Madama to the Accademia delle Scienze from where it was moved to its current location in 1989. The ground floor of the exhibit in the Sala della Scultura displays bas-reliefs by the Greeks and Romans and also findings from many important excavations in Piedmont and the Pianura Padana (the plain between Turin and Venice), and from around the old Roman town of Segusio (Susa). The first floor has many beautiful Greek and Etruscan ceramics as well as a specialist Cypriot and prehistoric collection. Most notable is the impressive collection of silverware known as the *Marengo horde* unearthed only in 1928, which includes the bust of Lucius Verus from 161-69 AD.

Via Garibaldi
Map 2, C2-6, p252

Running due west from piazza Castello to piazza Statuto, the modern-day via Garibaldi was the former *decumanus* or central horizontal street of the Roman settlement of Augusta Taurinorum. The street's old name was 'Dora Grossa' after the stream, used as a sewer, that used to run along the centre of the road. Today, as part of the revived area of the quadrilatero, via Garibaldi is a vibrant pedestrian street, full of bars, shops and the odd street act.

The quadrilatero
Map 2, B-C 2-5, p252

Bound in by Corso Valdocco to the west, via Garibaldi to the south, Corso Regina Margherita to the north and piazza Cesare Augusto to the east is the area known as the *quadrilatero romano*. The vestiges of the old Roman settlement, the tight network of streets still evoke the earthy atmosphere if not of a Roman town, then certainly of the Middle Ages. Until 10 years ago this was an unkempt area of the city. The local council offered incentives to firms to reinhabit what were always fine buildings and Turin's young entrepreneurial population obliged. Since then the area has become one of the city's trendiest and most bohemian. By night and day you can explore Turin's dialect on the global trend of concept bars and fusion restaurants, together with exhibition spaces and unusual shops.

Chiesa dei Santi Martiri
via Garibaldi 25, **T** 011 5622581. *0800-1200, 1500-1900.*
Map 2, C/D5, p252

Dedicated to the patron saints of Turin, Solutor, Adventor and Octavius, the interior is richly furnished with bronze, marble and stucco work and has a fine 19th-century frescoed vault by Luigi Vacca. The high altar was designed by Filippo Juvarra while the beautiful sacristy has a frescoed vault by Michele Antonio Milocco and lovely wood carvings.

Chiesa della Santissima Trinita
via Garibaldi 6/corner via XX Settembre, **T** 011 5156340. *0800-1200, 1500-1900. Map 2, C6, p252*

Set on the elegant pedestrian street of via Garibaldi is Chiesa della Santissima Trinita, both the design and burial place of Ascanio Vitozzi. Commissioned by the confraternity of the Santissima Trinita, it was completed between 1598-1606, although the neoclassical façade by Angelo Marchini was added in 1830. Inside, the circular plan was decorated in typical grand style by Filippo Juvarra, while the frescoes in the dome are by Luigi Vacca and date from 1844. The main altar dates from the turn of 17th century by Francesco Aprile after designs by Michelangelo Garove.

Palazzo di Città
piazza Palazzo di Città. *Map 2, C4/5, p252*

Turin's stately town hall is set in the middle of the 18th-century piazza Palazzo di Città (which used to be known as piazza delle Erbe). It was built between 1659-63 on the site of the medieval town hall to a design by Francesco Lanfranchi. It was subsequently enlarged and altered but the staircase, the *sale del sindaco* (the mayor's room) and the *sala del consiglio* (council room) still have their original 17th-century decorations. At the centre of the piazza stands a monument to il Conte Verde, Amedeo VI of Savoy by Pelagio Palagi, built in 1853.

Chiesa del Corpus Domini
via Palazzo di Città 20, **T** 011 4366025. *0800-1200, 1500-1900.*
Map 2, C5, p252

This church is built on the site of a miracle. On June 6, 1453, a soldier was trying to sell stolen goods from the Church of Exille in the Susa Valley when a host fell out of his bag and rose up of its own accord into the sky. According to one version of the story, the host then flew to the Bishop Ludovico di Romano. The first stone was not laid until 1603 but the exact site of the miracle is marked by a stone and surrounded by bars. The original plans were drawn up by Ascanio Vitozzi but of these only the façade with marble statues by Bernardo Falconi was realized. The most beautiful aspect of this small single-aisled little church is the delicate carving of the confessionals and choir stalls.

Chiesa di San Domenico
via San Domenico, **T** 011 5229711.   0800-1200, 1500-1900.
Map 2, B5, p252

At the intersection with via Milano, the church of Saint Dominic is the only gothic building in Turin. Built in the early 14th century, it was almost totally overhauled in 1776, while the beautiful façades, with tracery, rose windows and pinnacled buttresses from the 19th century are the work of Alfredo d'Andrade and Riccardo Braida. The jewel of the interior is the 1637 *Madonna of the Rosary* and *St Domenic and Catherine of Siena* by Guercino in the Chapel of the Rosary, framed by carved panels. The other altars feature paintings and frescoes by various Piemontese masters while in the Cappella della Madonna delle Grazie chapel is a spectacular sequence of frescoes from the 14th century by Maestro di San Domenico.

Piazza Repubblica
Map 2, A-B 5, p252

Beyond the Porta Palatina, piazza Repubblica, designed by Lorenzo Lombardi in 1814, is the largest square in Turin. It is less an elegant European enclosed space and more a wide open area reminiscent of north African cities. It is fitting that this square should host Turin's largest weekly fruit and veg market, also great for bargain leather-ware and household goods. Piazza Repubblica can be rather louche and it is best to watch your pockets, although efforts have been made to clear it up. At its southern end, piazza Repubblica becomes **piazza Porta Palazzo,** which together with its central porticoed avenue, via Milano, was designed by Filippo Juvarra in 1722.

The Cottolengo complex
Map 2, A2, p252

West of piazza Repubblica is the *Piccola Casa della Divina Provvidenza*, known as the Cottolengo complex after Giuseppe Benedetto Cottolengo who founded this hospital/school/home for the city's poor and sick in 1832. Cottolengo was canonized in 1934. Next to this stands the *Istituto Salesiano (Valdocco)*, a school for orphans founded by Giovanni Bosco in the 19th century. Bosco was also later canonized and his body is kept in the Chiesa di Santa Maria Ausiliatrice.

Chiesa di Santa Maria Ausiliatrice

via Maria Ausiliatrice 12, **T** 011 5224253. *0800-1200, 1500- 900.*
Map 2, A1, p252

Over 6,000 relics, including a piece of wood reported to part of the
Holy Cross, are conserved in the crypt of this huge domed church.
The frescoes in the cupola are by Giuseppe Rollin while the rest of
the marble interior is rich in paintings including many by Carlo
Morgari and Tommaso Maria Lorenzone, notably that which sits
over the main altar.

Borgo Dora and il Balon

Map 2, A4, p252

Every week on Saturday the area around via Borgo Dora, the north
of piazza Repubblica and the little streets off it is the scene of
Turin's flea market, known as *il Balon* (or sometimes *il Balôn*). The
old, the new and the innovative can be found here in twisting
street after street of shops and stalls in front of characterful houses
with iron filigree verandas, and cafés and bistros. There has been a
flea market recorded in Turin as far back as 1735 and it was
eventually consigned to this area in 1856. The showpiece market,
and in fact the largest open-air flea market in Europe, comprising
over 200 stalls, is the **Gran Balon**, which takes place on every
second Sunday of the month. More information on the market is
available from *Associazione Commericianti Balon, via Borgo Dora,*
T 011 4369741, www.balon.it (Italian only). Further north still along
via Valprato beyond and among the warehouses of Turin's Dora
station is another of Turin's post-industrial revitalized areas. Known
as **Docks Dora**, this former industrial park is a hot spot of
nightclubs, late lounges and jazz bars.

> **!** Il Balon/Balôn is so called because this was a district of the
> **•** city where street football was played in medieval times.

⭐ Black magic haunts

Best

- Basilica di Superga, p60
- Capella della Sacra Sindone, p45
- Murazzi, p54
- Museo Egizio, p67
- Piazzetta Reale, p44

Chiesa della Confraternita del Santo Sudario
Corner of via Piave 14 and via San Domenico 28, **T** 011 436832.
0800-1200, 1500-1900. Map 2, C3, p252

This church, built in 1734, is a fine example of Piedmontese rococo.
The most important feature as far as visitors to Turin are concerned
will probably be the museum in the crypt, **il Museo della Santa
Sindone** devoted to the study of the Holy Shroud of Turin.

Museo della Santa Sindone
via San Domenico 28, **T** 011 4365832, www.sindone.it *Open daily
0900-1200, 1500-1900. €6.16. Map 2, C3, p252*

Set in the church of the Confraternita del Santo Sudario, the
Museum of the Holy Shroud traces the history and conclusions of
the scientific tests carried out on the cloth since 1898 with a
collection of the various instruments and cameras that have been
used in examining, testing and dating the famous cloth. This is
accompanied by photographs, votive pieces of artwork and various
other documentation attesting to its history and veracity or other.
There is also a specialist library on the study area and it is the seat
of the *Centro Sindonologico Internazionale*, a body of scientists,
lawyers, engineers and theologians set up to study the shroud. It's
worth a visit to see how it balances religion and myth with science,
truth and fiction – not something you'd ever see in Rome...

Santuario della Consolata

piazza della Consolata, **T** 011 4363235. *0800-1200, 1500-1900.*
Map 2, C3, p252

Set in the picturesque little square of piazza della Consolata, the
original structure of this church goes back to the 5th century as a
place of worship dedicated to Saint Andrew. Worship of Maria
Consolatrice (Our Lady of Consolation – a blind man from
Briancon discovered the lost painting of the Madonna in 1104
which is usually on display and at the same time recovered his
sight) began in the 12th century and the church is devoted to
both. The building was erected in 1678 on a design by Guarini
and was expanded by Filippo Juvarra, who added the presbytery,
and later Carlo Ceppi at the turn of the 19th century. As such the
church bears all the hallmarks of Turin's most emblematic
architects. The church is accessed through the neoclassical portal
to the left of the Romanesque campanile.

Chiesa del Carmine

via del Carmine 3, **T** 011 4369525. *0800-1200, 1500-1900.*
Map 2, C3, p252

Designed by Filippo Juvarra, this church was built between 1732-36
and the current façade by Carlo Patarelli was added in 1872,
although the whole structure has been significantly restored after
suffering heavy bomb damage in the Second World War. After so
many lugubrious church interiors, the inside here with its galleried
side chapels is refreshingly bright. Adorning the apse is a painting,
the *Madonna e il Santo Amedeo di Savoia*, completed between
1755-60 by Beaumont while in the third chapel on the right is a
pretty depiction of the Immaculate Conception with the prophet
Elijah by Corrado Giaquinto.

Via della Consolata
Map 2, B3, p252

This elegant road is flanked by a number of private residences, former *case nobili* (homes of noble families), that are notable examples of the Turin baroque style.

Palazzo Falletti di Barolo
via delle Orfane 7, T 011 4360311.   *Mon, Wed 1000-1200, 1500-1700, Fri 1000-1200, closed Tue, Thu, Sat and Sun.* € *3.10. Currently only the Juvarra-designed hall is accessible to the public. Map 2, B4, p252*

This beautiful palace was expanded in 1692 by Gian Francesco Baroncelli. Here, the Italian patriot Silvio Pellico was received on being released from the Spielberg prison in 1830. The interior has beautiful inlaid 17th-century ceilings and baroque furnishings and decoration by Benedetto Alfieri dating to the 1740s.

Parco Pellerina
Winter 0900-1700, summer 0800-2200.   Map 1, E1, p250

Providing a verdant entrance into the northwest of the city from the airport, the parco Pellerina, recently re-named the parco Mario Carrara but still known as *la Pellerina*, is Italy's largest urban park. More of a rambling and rather worn strawy expanse of grass than a landscaped garden, the park is a favourite place for Sunday strolls, when you can see fathers walking along ignoring their wives and children as they listen to the football on portable radios. By night it is a less salubrious haunt of Turin's prostitutes and curb-crawlers.

A tale of *gobbi* and *drughi*

Known as the 'old lady' of Italian football, Juventus is the oldest of Turin's two football teams. It is also by far the more famous and most widely supported of Italian clubs on account of its stranglehold on the Italian Serie A championship, *lo scudetto*. Juventus have won 27 *scudetti* in total, more than any other Italian team by a country mile. The two gold stars on their distinctive 'bianconero' (black and white) strip bear testimony to this feat, one gold star equating to 10 championship victories. Juventus' European record is no less impressive and in 1985 they became the first club to win all three European trophies.

The list of great players that have graced the Stadio delle Alpi turf reads like a World XI: Roberto Baggio, Michel Platini, Dino Zoff, Zinedine Zidane, Gianluca Vialli, Edgar Davids, Gianluigi Buffon. Occasionally the odd British player has managed to squeeze in, but with limited success: Ian Rush and David Platt were left on the periphery, while Liam Brady was perhaps the most successful export. There is also a bizarre link to Stanley Kubrick's film, *A Clockwork Orange*, whose bullyish cast also wear black and white. Indeed, as the graffiti all over Turin bears testament, Juve fans refer to themselves as 'drughi' (from the Russian for 'friends'), a clear reference to the film. Fans of Toro (or in fact any other team) refer to Juve fans less pleasantly as 'gobbi' (hunchback) – but nobody seems to know exactly why.

Stadio delle Alpi
Map 1, C1, p250

Generally considered to be a bottomless drain on public money on a par with London's Millennium Dome, the Stadio delle Alpi was

Keeping out the riff-raff
The gilded gates of one of Turin's many stately homes.

built in time for the World Cup in 1990 and is Turin's main sports stadium. A magnificent structure, the stadium was criticized from the outset for lacking atmosphere, largely due to the athletics track which sets fans too far back from the pitch. During the winter there is sometimes too much atmosphere, with alpine fog descending so far that the pitch, let alone the players and the ball, is all but invisible from the grandstand. But for the time being this is where the home games of both Juventus and Torino FC are played. As part of Turin's overhaul for the 2006 Winter Olympics there are plans to knock down the stadium and concentrate Turin's sporting activities in a new stadium and a revamped Stadio Comunale.

Castles and country retreats

*Not satisfied with engineering the architecture of central Turin to their aristocratic taste, the Savoy Dukes also made sure that they had the country retreats to suit. When they fancied a bit of shooting and riding they had the **Stupinigi hunting lodge**; when a little privacy was needed there was the **Racconigi** or the **Castello della Mandria**. Thus to the north, south and west of Turin are a collection of country residences that were the envy of Europe's royal families. In 1997, the castles around Turin were designated a UNESCO World Heritage Site.*

◉ Sights

Palazzina di Caccia di Stupinigi
piazza Principe Amedeo 7, Nichelino, Torino, **T** 011 3581220, *www.mauriziano.it   Tue-Sun 1000-1700, closed Mon. € 6.20 adults, € 2.58 concessions   Map 4, p256*

At the end of Corso Unione Sovietica, the suburbs of Turin give way to green countryside. This is where the Savoy king, Vittorio Amedeo II had his hunting lodge built, commissioning his favourite architect, Filippo Juvarra to design it for him. By moonlight and on clear days, the villa's icon, a stag mounted on the central copper dome, is visible from quite some distance. More of a palace than a hunting lodge, the building is a typical Savoy combination of Louis XIV French and Italian baroque styles. The palace is set in ample grounds inhabited by deer while the immediate gardens are landscaped along classic symmetrical English lines. In total, 50 rooms are open to the public and together they constitute the **Museo di Storia, arte e ammobiliamento** (Museum of History, Art and Interior Design). Literally no expense was spared in furnishing these rooms which bring together marble fireplaces, lavish stuccoes and frescoes, gold leaf, exquisite marquetry, priceless carpets and unique pieces of furniture to create an ensemble of breathtaking operatic splendour.

Moncalieri
Map 4, p256

A virtual suburb of Turin, Moncalieri sits at 219 m atop the Collina Torinese embankment. Originally a separate Roman settlement, it is set out on two levels, the modern symmetrical lower town a prelude to the narrower winding streets of the higher old town. By far the town's most notable landmarks are the immense Colditz-like hulk of the **Castello Reale**, *piazza Baden Baden* **T** *011 641303, Thu, Sat, Sun 0830-1830, €2,* complete with turrets and a pavilion on each of its four corners and the church of Santa Maria della Scala. The castle was a 15th-century residence of the House of Savoy converted into the baroque style in 1619 by Carlo di Castellamonte and subsequently by Andrea Costaguta and Amedeo di Castellamonte. The interior was fitted out by the other Savoy favourites, Juvarra and Benedetto Alfieri. Today, a portion of the castle is home to the local constabulary but the royal apartments can still be visited in all their baroque splendour.

    Unusual in Turin's church-scape, **Santa Maria della Scala** is a fine example of Lombard Gothic style, although the entrance dates from the 17th century, and the balustrade is a 19th- century

Hunting and haunting

The stag atop the Stupinigi hunting lodge inspires thoughts of black magic.

addition. Beautifully restored inside, the church contains a carved organ loft and choirstalls. At the altar is *Our Lady of the Assumption* by Claudio Francesco Beaumont and in the first left-side chapel a lovely 15th-century terracotta *Pieta*.

Reggia di Venaria Reale and parco della Mandria

piazza della Repubblica 4, Venaria Reale, **T** 011 496272/4593675, *www.parks.it/parcomandria www.reggiavenariareale.it Castle: Tue, Thu, Sat 0900-1130, 1430-1730, other days by appointment only. € 5. Map 4, p256*

The vision of vast wilderness of this park was once the envy of Louis XIV and it is thought that the Reggia Veneria Reale was the inspiration behind Versailles. The Parisian version is more famous and thus the Reggia is sometimes known as *il Versailles Torinese*. Nowadays, it covers a mere half its former extent but is no less impressive. It is popular for strolls on Sundays, picnics and bike rides.

In terms of architecture, the **Reggia** (or royal palace) was conceived as a shrine to Diana, the goddess of hunting, a very royal pursuit. Don't miss the stunning and fully restored **Salone di Diana**, a breathtaking sight if you're into art. Beyond the **Torre dell'Orologio** (clock tower) in the piazza Repubblica, visitors accede to the main courtyard, the **Cortile Aulico del Cervo**, below which stretch the lower gardens and ponds. Not many of the former royal buildings in the main complex of the Reggia are open to the public but the **Galleria Diana** and **Cappella di Sant-Uberto**, designed by Juvarra, give an idea of the former royal extravagance. The rest of the buildings such as the **Scuderie** (stables) and **Citroneria** (orangerie) are due to reopen to the public in 2005/6.

The **Parco de la Mandria**, via Carlo Emanuele II 256, **T** 011 4993322, *Apr-Sept 0800-2000, Oct-Nov 0800-1800, Nov-Feb 0800-1700*, is reached from the Reggia by via Amedeo di Savoia. Formerly the grazing ground of the horses of the Reggia, it has a number of important buildings, most notably the **Castello della Mandria** (or **Palazzina Reale**), via Carlo Emanuele II 256, Venaria Reale, **T** 011 4993322, € 5.16, visits by appointment only, the work of Juvarra and Alfieri, and the apartments where Vittorio Emanuele II lived with his morganatic wife, 'la Bella Rosina'. Don't forget also the beautiful 13th-century church of **San Giuliano,** the **Castello dei Laghi** mini castle from 1860 and the 19th-century country villas of **Ville Peroncini e Ghia**.

Castello di Rivoli

piazza Mafalda di Savoia, Rivoli, **T** 011 9565220, www.castellodirivoli.org *Tue-Thu 1000-1700, Fri-Sun 1000-2200, Mon closed. €6.20. There is a shuttlebus from piazza Castello (corner via Po) on Sat and Sun, € 2. Map 4, p256*

The culmination of corso Francia due west of Turin is the historically important medieval fortress-town of Rivoli, sitting atop an outcrop at 390-m above sea level. Surveying the surrounding plain is the **Castello**, a stiff climb but with superb panoramic views. Originally built in the 11th century, the Savoy dukes turned the Rivoli Castle into one of their many sumptuous country residences in the 13th century. Various architects were commissioned to work on the project, causing a sequence of styles to be superimposed on top of one an other. Under Napoleonic rule the castle fell into disrepair, and finally became public property in 1883. The building was given a new lease of life in 1979 when it was transformed into the fantastic and highly recommended **Museo d'Arte Contemporanea**. It is a fusion of ancient and modern, exhibiting works of photography and short films in rooms evocative of their lavish 16th- and 17th-century past. The exhibition includes works by Hans Richter, Gilbert and George, William Morris and Anselm Kiefer.

Castello di Racconigi
via Morosini 1/piazza Carlo Alberto, Racconigi (Cuneo), **T** 0172 84005. *Park: Apr-Oct Sun and public holidays 1000 until 1 hr before sunset, € 2. Castle: Tue-Sun 0830-1930. € 5. Entry to castle and park € 6. Map 4, p256*

Due south of Turin beyond the Stupinigi hunting lodge is the beloved out-of-town residence of Carlo Alberto, an enormous and splendid red-brick palace decorated with marble baroque flourishes. The original building dates back to the 12th century and was transformed into another of the Savoys' royal palaces by Guarino Guarini. However, it was the Bolognese architect Pelagio Palagi who really left his mark on the construction. Inside are a number of wonderfully decadent rooms such as the **Grande Salone**, full of stucco, statues and gold, the **Salone di Diana**, characterized by 18th-century bas-reliefs and the **Appartamento Cinese**, hung with valuable oriental wall coverings. Other rooms display paintings by the hands of artists such as Francesco Beaumont, Claude Dauphin and Jan Miel. Palazzo Racconigi stands in 170 ha of park with undulations, lakes, streams and waterfalls added in the 19th century as well as the neogothic farmhouse, **La Margherita**. The gardens contain a number of other small and intriguing outhouses such as the **Palazzina Svizzera** (Swiss Cottage) from 1890, pheasant pen and stables.

Castello Ducale di Aglié

piazza Castello 2, Aglié, **T** 0124 330102. *Castle: Tue-Sun 0830-1830, closed Mon, € 4. Park: Tue-Sun 0900-1300, 1400-1900, € 2. Entry to Park and Castle € 5. Map 4, p256*

Twenty or so km north of Turin, Aglié is an attractive and romantic little medieval town notable for the baroque **Chiesa di Santa Maria** and its fine 300-room ducal palace. In 1391 the town passed into the hands of the Savoys who turned the original 12th-century castle from a stronghold into a residential palace. The palace sits in 32 ha of lush verdant grounds landscaped in the English style, punctuated by marble statues and, at their centre, a beautiful 18th-century water fountain depicting the Dora flowing into the Po. Only 18 of the 300 rooms can be visited but they give an indelible impression of aristocratic style and luxury, in particular the wonderful stuccoed and frescoed ballroom, the small art gallery in room six and the *Sala dei Monumenti Archeologici* which contains many Etruscan, Greek and Roman objects.

Le Langhe

*Thirty or so miles southeast of Turin the plain rises into a series of undulating hills beautifully raked with the symmetrical parallel lines of vineyards, suggestive of fertility, fruit and well-being. These are the hills of Le Langhe, the region known for producing the most famous of Italian wines, **Barolo**, as well as the lighter **Nebbiolo** and the staple, quaffable **Dolcetto**. This is also the land of the white truffle and a visit to the area is a gastronome's delight, even more so if you're into* lumache *(snails), which are a regional speciality. The capital of the region is the pretty town of **Alba**. If you're there in October, don't miss the **donkey race** or the town's **truffle festival** in the same month. The wine-making villages south of Alba are pretty and earthy and it is possible to taste and buy great wines direct from small and medium-size producers.*

▸▸ *See Sleeping p131, Eating and drinking p161*

◉ Sights

Alba

Map 4, p256

Alba is not linked to Turin by rail and only infrequently by bus so it is best to explore the area with a private vehicle. For tourist office information, see p29.

The capital of the region is the pretty town of **Alba**, still with its medieval red-brick towers which rise above the town and announce it from afar. Within the cobbled streets of the town itself are a number of interesting baroque and Renaissance palazzi and, on piazza Risorgimento, a beautifully restored **Duomo** containing beautiful Renaissance stalls. The streets are lined with gourmet shops and mouth-watering restaurants

Aperitif time

Cinzano, made 10 km west of the nearby town of Alba, is enjoyed with customary platefuls of appetisers in Turin's busy bars

which means that Alba – where they make Nutella and Ferrero Rocher chocolates – is more a place to eat, drink and spoil yourself than somewhere to be distracted by anything too cultural. The only exceptions are visits in October to see the **donkey race**, a parody of the Palio horserace in the nearby rival town of Asti, or for the serious business of the town's **truffle festival** where you can spend a fortune on a knobbly nugget of delectably whiffy mushroom.

Around Alba
Map 4, p256

The aperitif Cinzano is made in the eponymous village 10 km west of Alba, while south of Alba are the wine-making villages of **Barolo** itself, **Annunziata**, **La Morra** and **Grinzane di Cavour**, each pretty, rural and earthy and with excellent restaurants and wineries.

In Barolo, the **Enoteca Regionale del Barolo** in the village castle on piazza Falletti is a good place to taste and buy wine, **T** 0173 56277, *open daily for tasting except Thu.*

Asti and around

Around Turin

*The Roman town of Asti will forever have associations, at least among British readers, with cheap, not always drinkable, sparkling wine, for it is here since the mid-19th century that the grapes have been cultivated to make that staple of student parties, **Asti Spumante**. Consumed in its home environment, preferably young and chilled, Asti Spumante is a much better drink, unrecognizable from the brew which reaches the local off-licence at home. Wine apart, a good reason to visit Asti is its **Palio horse race**, full of medieval pagentry. Beyond Asti to the east is **Alessandria**, a plain and industrial provincial town while **Acqui Terme** next door is a Roman spa town with a spring in the main piazza.*

▸▸ *See Sleeping p133, Eating and drinking p162*

◉ Sights

Asti
Map 4, p256

Asti and Alessandria are on the Turin-Genoa rail route, linked by frequent trains in both directions. The journey to Asti takes around an hour, to Alessandria 15 mins more. By road these towns are reached by the A21, the Autostrada dei Vini (the wine motorway). For tourist office information, see p30.

Wine aside, a good reason to visit Asti is its **Palio** horse race on the third Sunday in September, no less lavish than its more famous relative in Siena. Otherwise, Asti is a quiet town and the Campo del Palio is nothing more than a car park for the rest of the year. There is little remarkable culture aside from the main church, the **Collegiata di San Secondo**, dedicated to Asti's patron saint, on the central piazza Alfieri, a fine example of early gothic with a sixth-century crypt. South of Asti is **Costigliole d'Asti**, the heart of Spumante country and nearby the **Abbazia di Vezzolano**, a Romanesque abbey allegedly founded by Charlemagne, said to have had a vision here in the eighth-century. The virtues of the spring in neighbouring **Acqui Terme** are celebrated in the writings of Pliny and Seneca. The aqueduct is the only remaining trace of Roman presence.

The Val de Susa

*The Val de Susa and the surrounding tributary valleys are the reason why Turin was chosen to host the 2006 Winter Olympics. The once glamorous now rather over-developed ski resorts of **Sestriere**, **San Sicario** and **Sauze d'Oulx** will host the lion's share of the alpine events, while other villages and resorts such as **Bardonecchia**, **Cesana**, **Claviere** and **Pragelato** will host events such as ski-jumping, biathlon, bobsleigh and the skating championships.*

▸▸ *See Sleeping p133, Eating and drinking p163*

◉ Sights

Susa
Map 4, p256

Susa is the main transport link with Turin, well served by buses and the motorway to the Frejus tunnel. The journey takes around 40 mins. Departure and fare information is available from the Turin and Susa tourist offices, see p30.

This is a real Turin weekender destination, perfect for letting off steam without the attention to rural tradition and nature of, say the Val d'Aosta. That said, the town of **Susa**, although a little earthy and rough, has its own charm. It was originally an old Celtic town, which held out, Asterix-style, against the prevailing Roman wind, under the Gaulish leader, Cottius. There are a number of remains from Gallo-Roman times, most notably the no-nonsense defensive gate on **piazza San Giusto**, some vestiges of the **Roman baths** in the central park and the **Arco d'Augusto** arch erected by Cottius in honour of the Roman emperor. The most worthwhile detour in the area is found just before Susa at the **Sacra di San Michele**, **T** 011 939130, a Dracula-esque abbey spookily perched on an outcrop and reached from either the ugly village of Avigliana or the more atmospheric approach of Sant'Ambrogio, via a precarious set of steps hewn into the rock. They are appropriately named *La Scala dei Morti*, not because of the number of tourists who have tumbled to an untimely death, but because this is where the monks used to lay out the dead for the local peasantry to come and pay their last respects. Equally forbidding and at the end of the Susa Valley, 70 km from Turin, is the **Forte di Exilles**, **T** 01225 58270, a medieval fortress which was used as a military installation right through to the Second World War.

Saluzzo

While many of Turin's surrounding towns are notable mainly for their proximity to nature, castles and monasteries, Saluzzo is a refreshing exception in that it is beautiful in its own right. Situated about 60 km south of Turin, it is an immaculately preserved medieval town that, were it not for its modern trappings, would be a trip back in time.

▸▸ *See Sleeping p134, Eating and drinking p163*

Sights

Saluzzo
Map 4, p256

Saluzzo is connected by bus with Turin. The journey takes roughly 90 mins. Departure times and fares can be obtained from Turin and Saluzzo tourist offices. By car take the A6 and exit at Bra then take the SS20. For tourist information, see p30.

Saluzzo was a fiercely independent town in the Middle Ages until it was signed over to the Savoys in 1601 in a treaty with France. Today, twisting cobblestone streets lead up to a forbidding castle, **la Castaglia**, while little piazzas are flanked by Renaissance palazzi frescoed with trompe l'oeil landscapes. From the castle and from the **Torre Civica**, a 15th-century tower, visitors can look down on postcard-worthy red-tiled roofs and the surrounding valleys and plain. The 16th-century **Museo Civico di Casa Cavassa**, *Tue-Sun 1000-1300, 1400-1800, € 3.50*, is laid out with the furnishing of a *casa nobile* of the period, including a beautiful, golden picture of the Madonna protecting the population of Saluzzo. Just out of town is another castle, the **Castello di Manta**, equally forbidding as la Castaglia, which is worth entering to admire a fine sequence of Gothic frescoes. The Saluzzo Valley stretches west, defined by the tooth of the Mon Viso, Piedmont's highest peak. Mountaineers intent on conquering Mon Viso should head for **Crissolio** where a short hike leads up to the Pian del Re at the Po's source. The tunnel at Pertuis de la Traversette is alleged to be the point where Hannibal crossed the Alps with his elephants. Non-mountaineers can still enjoy beautiful treks through plunging valleys and round glistening icy mountain lakes.

The Val d'Aosta

*The stunning Aosta Valley is crowned by some of the most famous mountains in the Alps, **Mont Blanc**, the **Matterhorn** and **Monte Rosa**, whose rugged faces, glaciers and alternately snow-laden and lush green slopes offer a year-round paradise for skiers, climbers and hikers. In the opening credits of* The Italian Job *Beckermann drives round the winding roads of the Aosta Valley before meeting his end at the hands of the Mafia. A wealthy and autonomous region within Italy where bilingualism in French and Italian is law, the Val d'Aosta has a strong and very singular identity. Italian was only introduced with the Risorgimento in 1861 and the most commonly heard dialect here is an Alpine mix of Italian, German and French owing to the region's original Swiss descendants.*

▸▸ *See Sleeping p134, Eating and drinking p163*

 Sights

The valley
Map 4, p256

Aosta is 90 mins by bus or train from Turin, served by 7 or 8 trains daily from Porta Susa and from the main bus station. The A5 motorway now runs all the way to the French border. A single fare costs around € 20. All information on local bus and train routes in the Val d'Aosta and on accommodation, trails and hikes in the surrounding valleys can be obtained from the Aosta tourist office, see p30.

Until the advent of the Romans, the area was populated by a tribe known as the Salassi. When Emperor Augusta threw them out in 25 BC, the main settlement, **Aosta** (a corruption of the word 'Augusta') was re-christened after him and since then the valley has been coveted for its important route through the Alps, now plied daily by hundreds of lorries through the Mont Blanc tunnel. In the Middle Ages the Val D'Aosta became part of the Kingdom of Bourgogne and thereafter Napoleonic France, ruled for seven centuries by the Challant family whose precipitously-placed Romanesque and Gothic feudal castles and fortifications provide breathtaking views. More spectacular than the main valley itself are Val d'Aosta's tributary valleys, peppered with pretty villages, more castles and a host of nature trails for the dilettante hiker and serious climbs for the experienced mountaineer. To the east lie the three picturesque valleys of Val Gressoney, with chocolate box scenery and the castles of **Verrès** and **Issogne**; **Val d'Ayas** with the chic ski resort of **Champoluc**; and **Valtournenche**, crowned by the **Matterhorn massif** and home to the ugly ski resort of **Cervinia** and the magnificent **Castello Fenis**. West of Aosta, the valley reaches out towards Switzerland by the famous **Col di San Bernardo** with its famous mountain pass and thick-coated St Bernard dogs, and to France via the Mont Blanc tunnel and the resorts of **Courmayeur** and **La Thuile**. Before the border, however, is the vast expanse of the **parco Gran Paradiso**, Italy's second largest national park providing almost limitless randonees on foot, cycle or crampon in the company of ibex and chamois.

Aosta

Map 4, p256

Sometimes ambitiously referred to as the 'Rome of the Alps', little remains of the original Roman military settlement. Most of Aosta's limited beauty is medieval and its key attraction is undoubtedly its location and usefulness as a springboard for exploration of the valleys. That said, there are a number of sights to delay the visitor such as the **Arco d'Augusto**, between the main gate of Porta Pretoria and the Roman bridge of the dried-up river Buthier. This is the triumphal arch erected to celebrate the ousting of the Salassi tribe and victory for Emperor Augustus. The effect of triumph is somewhat diminished by the addition of an incongruous 18th-century roof and the amount of traffic that zooms around it, but the mountain backdrop goes some way to compensating for this. The pair of triple-arched gateways that comprise the **Porta Pretoria** itself, on via Porta Pretoria, is an impressive relic of Roman occupation and the tower above houses temporary exhibitions. Aosta also has the vestiges of a **Roman theatre**, a four-storey arch-window façade and part of the auditorium where shows are still performed in summer, *daily 0900-1900 in summer, 0930-1200, 1430-1630 in winter, free*. There are also a couple of notable churches including the 10th-century **Chiesa di Sant'Orso** which contains some fine ceiling frescoes. You can visit the church via some perilous walkways in the company of the sacristan and some beautifully carved choir stalls; the cathedral on piazza Giovanni XXIII is also interesting with its neoclassical façade, gothic interior and two 12th-century mosaics. It also has a small museum annex, *0900-1900 daily, free*. Otherwise Aosta is no more than a pleasant alpine town. Most of the life is in the smart cafés and restaurants along via Sant'Anselmo. Between March and October you may be lucky to see one of the local cow fights, part of a yearly knock-out competition designed to find the queen of the cows called *La Bataille de la Reine*.

Ivrea
Map 4, p256

Ivrea lies about 50 km northwest of Turin and is easily accessible by all means of transport. By car take the swift A5 autostrada. This is also used by the regular bus service and the even more regular and cheaper (twice hourly) train service. Ivrea lies on the well-travelled route up to the Aosta Valley. Contact the Turin train and bus stations for fares and exact times. For tourist information, see p30.

Just under an hour north of Turin en route to the Val d'Aosta, Ivrea is a pretty riverside walled medieval town with, like most towns in the region, a formidable castle and the country's most riotous carnival. The Olivetti industry has its seat here and this, alongside other modern commercial success, has brought an uglier side to the outskirts of Ivrea.

In general, Ivrea is a town of cobbled streets, quiet cafés and smart restaurants. Quiet, that is, until carnival time when Ivrea wakes up in style, with one of Italy's most riotous but strangely, not widely-reported, **carnivals** when for three days the inhabitants of the town pelt each other with oranges. The tradition goes back to the Middle Ages when the local tyrant enforced his right to sleep with every maiden in town on their wedding night. In this he succeeded until the wedding of the miller's daughter – obviously the fairest maiden in the history of Ivrea – whose husband beheaded the tyrant while she was in bed with him. The blood oranges are meant to represent the rolling head of the tyrant. In practice for the three days leading up to Mardi Gras, the windows and façades of the town's three squares are covered in protective netting. During these days between 0900 and 1700, chariots of locals dressed in the colours of the former ruling aristocratic families wheel through the squares, each drawn by scarily masked protected horses, like riot police, and rain down oranges on the populace. If you are wearing a red beret (and as a tourist you can buy one and join in) you have the right to throw oranges back. It is fantastic anarchic fun and you will inevitably end up with a sore shoulder and also a black eye from the oranges, while under foot at the end of each day is a pulp of Sicilian oranges almost a foot deep, often mixed with snow. Highly recommended.

▸▸ *See Sleeping p135, Eating and drinking p164*

Valleys to the east
Map 4, p256

Val Gressoney is a *Sound of Music* vision of lush fields and wooden houses and chalets. The main villages are **Pont St Martin** which provides the rail and bus link from Aosta and beyond that the villages of **Gressoney-St-Jean** and **Gressoney-la-Trinite**, both of which provide bases for lovely excursions such as up to the mountain lake at Gabiet and the peak of Valsesia and on to Biel, the home of one of the original Walser settlements from Switzerland where their native dialect of German is still spoken.

The symbol of the valley of Val d'Ayas is the peak of **Monte Rosa**, surveying a beautiful wide open valley of dense woodland. At its heart is the ski resort of **Champoluc**, providing enjoyable intermediate slopes and is more interesting for serious climbers who will want to scale the daunting Testa Grigia. The village of Brusson provides the best base for this here.

At the heart of the valley, set on a rocky outcrop is the castle of **Castello Verrès**, *0900-1900 Mar-Nov, 0900-1230, 1400-1730 Oct-Feb, closed Wed, guided tours every half hour*, a bare and forbidding construction, actually unspectacular were it not for its situation. A bare castle on a bare mountain, it was built as a military fortress by Ibelto di Challant, the spartans soldiers' quarters testifying to the austere conditions. Ironically though, the castle is supposed to be one of the first to have had a toilet installed.

Further on, the 15th-century **Castello d'Issogne**, *0900-1900 Mar-Nov, 0900-1230, 1400-1730 Oct-Feb, guided tours every half hour*, is more lavish and interesting, as it was a residence for the Challant family overlords. A short walk from the bus stop at Verrès, it appears unspectacular from outside but the interior is preserved in the style of a gothic ducal residence with an arcaded courtyard and a rich selection of frescoes.

Valtournenche
Map 4, p256

What could and should have been Val'Aosta's most stunning valley has been ruined by thoughtless development, no worse than in the functional blocks of the resort of **Breuil-Cervinia** at the foot of the 4,467 m **Matterhorn** (known to Italians as *Il Cervino*). One of Italy's first ski resorts and commissioned by Mussolini, it now provides very mediocre skiing, albeit with a great view, on parched south-facing slopes that are often patchy. The main benefit is that skiers can ski down into **Zermatt** on the (prettier) Swiss side and see the mountain as it looks on a box of Alpen cereal.

Saving the valley from this disappointing impression is the **Castello Fenis**, *0900-1900 Mar-Nov, 0900-1230, 1400-1730 Oct-Feb, guided tours every half hour*, a magnificently restored Camelot-style fairytale of follies, towers, crenellations and turrets nestled among wooded hills. It is no surprise to learn that the castle was conceived for the aesthetic effect and to exercise the vanity of the Challant family with the defense of the valley left to the fortress at Nus.

Valleys to the west
Map 4, p256

West of Aosta, the road leads to the Mont Blanc tunnel, which has now recently reopened following a fire in 1997 which killed 37 people. Above the tunnel rise the peaks of **Mont Blanc** and the **Aiguille du Midi**, the highest point of the ski resort of Chamonix and a favourite of expert skiers and climbers.

Due north of Aosta is the road to the mountain pass of the **Col di San Bernardo** into Switzerland. The pass was named after the monastery that provided shelter for travellers and which also gave its name to the cuddly but dopey St Bernard dogs who became famous as mountain rescuers (albeit with a drop of whisky).

The road and railway west lead to the parco Nazionale del Gran Paradiso, passing on its way a number of famous castles. A short walk from the station of St Maurice is the **Castello di Sarre**, a 13th-century construction recently restored and significantly restyled by King Vittorio Emanuele II. It was his out-of-town hunting lodge and he took care to festoon the interior with seemingly all of his antlered conquests. Legend has it he bought the wrong castle, preferring the Aymaville castle opposite but the agent mistook the direction of the river and got the wrong side. Further on is the **Castello di Saint-Pierre**, dating from the 12th century but restyled in the18th century with extravagant crenellations and turrets.

Parco Nazionale del Gran Paradiso
Map 4, p256

Italy's second largest park takes its name from the 4,061 m Gran Paradiso mountain which can be climbed from the village of Valsavarenche. The park was the project of King Vittorio Emanuele II, a passionate hunter who donated it to the Italian state in 1922. In doing so he ensured the survival of the local population of ibex so that, aside from those that now decorate the walls of his castles, an abundant population roam freely for the passive enjoyment of commoners. The park is split over three valleys, Cogne, Valsavarenche and Val de Rhemes, with Cogne and its cliffs, glaciers and rivers being at once the most spectacular and the main transport link with Aosta. The park provides an infinite choice of treks and hikes for all standards and in winter also some cross-country ski trails.

Wish you were here...

Turin's hilltop palaces and spires make the city visible from afar.

Sleeping

Turin has always been well stocked with hotels, however, until recently, accommodation was either rather functional and business-orientated or rather dreary. Nowadays, Turin's hoteliers are fully conversed in the style and comfort to which the international tourist has become accustomed. The hip or designer hotel fashion that arrived rather belatedly in Italy finds a dialect here, and 2005 is should see the opening of the city's first five-star hotel. Due to Turin's prominence as a business centre the better hotels are often busy so book as far in advance as you can. The tourist office on piazza Castello offers a free hotel reservation service if you book within 48 hours of your arrival. Many hotels offer discounts for staying the weekend or a minimum number of nights (T 011 4407032, 0930-1900, reshotel@turismotorino.org). Some discounts are also available to holders of the Torino Card but you won't necessarily be able to take advantage of this until you are in Turin and have the card.

€ Sleeping codes

Price

LL	€ 220 and over	D	€ 80-100
L	€ 200-220	E	€ 60-80
AL	€ 180-200	F	€ 40-60
A	€ 150-180	G	up to € 40
B	€ 120-150		
C	€ 100-120		

Prices are for a double room in high season.

The other thing worth noting is that, save for in the top-class hotels where you will be treated to a full smorgasbord of English and continental choice, breakfast is not big in Italy, neither in the size nor in the style of the portions. As most Italians believe in taking their breakfast (at most a brioche and a cappuccino) on the run, it is far better to identify a favourite café near your hotel and enjoy your coffee and croissant local-style, rather than sit suffering the lugubrious service and produce in your hotel in a rather anodine non-Italian environment.

If you are only in Turin for the weekend then the best areas to stay in, both for hotel architecture and proximity to the main sights and life of the city, are in the southeast and northwest within walking distance of piazza Castello. The hotels along Corso Vittorio Emanuele are also well-placed and pretty, if a little noisy when facing the street.

Central

F San Carlo, piazza San Carlo 197, **T** 011 5627846. Map 2, E7, p253 This hotel's lowly grading and cost belie its superb location overlooking Turin's most elegant square which makes it highly recommended. Accommodation is simple but clean and comfortable, and breakfast is available in one of the many cafés outside downstairs.

> ▶ **Torino weekend**
>
> Twenty-five of Turin's hotels, ranging from two- to four-star
> establishments, belong to a 'club' where €78 will get you two
> nights (minimum stay) for two people including breakfast and a
> Torino Card. Call the main tourist office at least seven days before
> arrival and quote the scheme to take advantage of the offer.

Southwest

B Hotel Parco Fiera, via Giordano Bruno 210, **T** 011 6197745,
F 011 6199562. *Map 1, J5, p251* If trendiness overrides your need
for central positioning or traditional elegance, this is a good option
in the stylish contemporary Lingotto neighbourhood. Twenty
rooms are clinically and stylishly furnished and finished with an
excess of modern comforts.

C Best Western Boston, via Massena 70, **T** 011 500359, **F** 011
599358, www.hotelbostontorino.it *Map 3, B5, p254* Despite being a
chain hotel, this is a good choice for romantics. 'The art of the hotel,
the hotel of art' so goes the hotel's slogan and the foyer and most of
the 91 rooms in this liberty/art nouveau palazzo display works of
contemporary art. Many rooms also have four-poster beds.

D Astoria, via XX Settembre 4, **T** 011 5620653. *Map 2, E6, p252*
Located in an elegant central townhouse typical of Turin this is a
convenient, good value and stylish address with all mod cons and
an inner garden for guests.

E Bologna, C.so Vittorio Emanuele 60, **T** 011 5620191. *Map 2, H4,
p252* A nice little hotel on one of Turin's grand boulevards with a
chirpy management. It is centrally located although the front
rooms can be noisy (or atmospheric, depending on your mood).

Northwest

A **City**, via Filippo Juvarra 25, **T** 011 540546, **F** 011 548188, cityhotel@iol.it *Map 2, D2, p252* Centrally located near Porta Susa station, this is one of Turin's new breed of design hotels characterized here by loud and contrasting colours in its 57 rooms. There is also a not particularly atmospheric bar.

A **Diplomatic**, via Cernaia 42, **T** 011 5612444, **F** 011540472, www.hotel-diplomatic.it *Map 2, E3, p252* Located conveniently 100 m from Porta Susa station, this is a modern and comfortable hotel belonging to the World Hotels SRS chain. It offers all mod cons on the one of the main elegant streets of the city with 123 rooms and a restaurant specializing in regional dishes.

Southeast

L **Jolly Hotel Principi di Piemonte**, via Gobetti 15, **T** 011 5577111, **F** 011 5620270. *Map 2, F7, p253* Backing onto via Roma, this hotel is in the thick of the city's cafés, boutiques and general action and is a long-standing classic in Turin. The 99 rooms and apartments are kitted out in full comfort.

L **Le Meridien Lingotto**, via Nizza 262, **T** 011 6642000, **F** 011 6642001, www.lemeridien-lingotto.it *Map 1, J6 p251* A little detached from the Turin of arcades, museums and shops, this is nevertheless the number one choice for guests for whom contemporary design and the latest in local accommodation fads is paramount. Unique despite being a chain hotel, the building is part of the conference centre complex in the former Fiat factory converted by the super-modern architect, Renzo Piano. All the 240 rooms are decorated in a minimalist style with design artifacts. The hotel also boasts a fitness centre and a decent restaurant.

L **Starhotel Majestic**, C.so Vittorio Emanuele II 54, **T** 011 539153, **F** 011 534963, www.starhotels.it *Map 2, G8, p253* Recently redecorated, the Starhotel has been elegantly furnished to resemble a 19th-century town house. It is popular with business travellers but leisure travellers will also be enchanted by the decor and in particular the refined *Le Regine* restaurant, illuminated by a glass atrium. Always nice for a late night drink in the piano bar.

A **Grand Hotel Sitea**, via Carlo Alberto 35, **T** 011 5170171, **F** 011 548090, www.thi.it *Map 2, E8, p253* The Sitea is a refined and elegant luxury hotel located in an 18th-century palazzo with an understated decor that oozes the manners and charm of times gone by. Besides the 118 spacious and warm rooms there is a bar resembling a gentleman's club and a fine and renowned restaurant, the *Carignano*, specializing in local dishes.

A **Jolly Hotel Ligure**, piazza Carlo Felice 85, **T** 011 55641, **F** 011 535438, www.jollyhotels.it *Map 2, G7, p253* Located in a fine 19th-century town house, this hotel is central, a short walk from Porta Nuova station and has many rooms overlooking the central, but sometimes less than salubrious, park in piazza Carlo Felice. Inside however, the rooms have been nicely refurbished and there is also a decent bar and restaurant.

A **Royal**, C.so Regina Margherita 249, **T** 011 4376777, **F** 011 4276393, www.hotelroyal.it *Map 2, A7, p253* Stuck out by the northern ring road, this hotel is geared principally towards the business traveller and is often used for conferences. Comfortable, modern and not particularly special, it is a useful fall-back if nothing central is available.

A **Turin Palace Hotel**, via Sacchi 8, **T** 011 5625511, **F** 011 5612187, www.thi.it *Map 2, H6, p252* The traditional choice for visiting celebrities, you might even be able to sleep on the same

> **Bed and breakfast**
> The local *Associazione Bed & Breakfast*, via dei Mille 23, T 011
> 8123810, can find you a room if you're looking for bed and
> breakfast in the city, although they only take bookings a
> maximum of seven days prior to arrival. *Turismo Torino* can
> also offer alternatives on T 011 4407032, www.turismotorino.org
> or reshotel@turismotorino.org

sheets as Madonna here. Failing that, the other 123 rooms of this
converted 19th-century palazzo will still satisfy any material girl.
There is also a respected restaurant, the *Vigna Reale*, which is
equally expert in the preparation of local specialities and
international dishes. As part of the *Turin Hotels International Group*,
guests should also be able to obtain specials deals in certain
restaurants such as *Ristorante del Cambio*, see p150.

B Concord, via Lagrange 47, **T** 011 5176756, **F** 011 5176305,
www.hotelconcord.com *Map 2, F7, p253* A comfortable and
quiet business hotel in plum centre with 139 well-appointed and
airy rooms, a reasonable restaurant, *Le Lanterne*, and good
business facilities.

B Jolly Hotel Ambasciatori, C.so Vittorio Emanuele II 104, **T** 011
5752, **F** 011 544978, www.jollyhotels.it *Map 2, G9, p253* A little
away from the action, this rather bland hotel is more business
focused but a comfortable option if needs be.

C Holiday Inn Turin City Centre, via Assietta 3, **T** 011 5167111,
F 011 5167699, www.holiday-inn.com *Map 2, H6, p252* Kitted out
like Holiday Inns around the world, so nothing spectacular, with
every modern comfort catered for in effortless mediocre style.

★ Hotels

- Des Artistes – for that bohemian touch, p130
- Dogana Vecchia – for atmosphere and a personal touch, p129
- Liberty – for a taste of art nouveau Turin, p130
- Meridien Lingotto – for contemporary design and luxury, p125
- Sitea – for elegant luxury, p126

C Roma & Rocca Cavour, piazza Carlo Felice 60, **T** 011 5612772. *Map 2, G6, p252* A grand 19th-century town house building with 93 rooms, located opposite the station. Convenient, comfortable and with nice views in the front rooms of the park below.

Northeast and Borgo Po

A Villa Sassi, strada Traforo del Pino 47, **T** 011 8980556, **F** 011 8980095, www.villasassi.com *Map 1, A8, p250* The 17th-century Villa Sassi is reputed to have been the former suburban refuge of King Victor Amadeus II, subsequently belonging to a sequence of noble torinese families before going the way of many such residences. Its position in a piece of parkland at the foot of the hill, on which the Superga basilica stands,makes it a quiet and agreeable alternative to the rumpus of the city.

C Best Western Genova & Stazione, via Sacchi 14, **T** 011 5629400, www.bestwestern.com *Map 3, A6, p254* Fifty-nine well-furnished and comfortable rooms set in an elegant turn of the century palazzo, conveniently situated next to Porta Nuova station.

C Best Western Luxor, C.so Stati Uniti 7, **T** 011 5620777, **F** 011 5628324, www.hoteluxor.it *Map 3, A5, p254* Eight floors of spacious modern rooms, some of which have jacuzzis, located near to Porta Nuova station.

C **Best Western Piemontese**, via Berthollet, **T** 011 6698101, **F** 011 6690571, www.hotelpiemontese.it *Map 3, A8, p255* The least remarkable of Best Western's Turin outposts although the smaller size, just 37 rooms, provides for a more personal touch. There is no restaurant although the hotel does offer breakfast.

C **Chelsea**, via XX Settembre 79/e, **T** 011 4360100, **F** 011 4363141, www.hotelchelsea.it *Map 2, F6, p252* One of Turin's rare family run hotels with 15 simple but comfortable rooms run with a personal homely attitude. The hotel also boasts an excellent restaurant, *La Campana*, run by the same family.

C **Conte di Biancamano**, C.so Vittorio Emmanuele II 73, **T** 011 5623281, **F** 011 5623789 www.venere.com/it/torino/biancamano *Map 2, H8, p253* The bright stuccoed, frescoed and chandeliered interior of the foyer should not deceive potential guests as the modern rooms above are comparatively disappointing. The small size, just 25 rooms, does make this an intimate choice. There is no restaurant.

C **Crimea**, via Mentana 3, **T** 011 6604700, **F** 011 6604912, www.hotelcrimea.it *Map 3, 12A, p255* South of the centre but within easy each by public transport of all the action, the Crimea is a modern hotel in a quiet residential district with 49 rooms, a neon-lit bar and conference facilities. Breakfast only.

C **Dogana Vecchia**, via Corte d'Appello 4, **T** 011 4366752, **F** 011 4367194 . *Map 2, C5, p252* Located in a former 17th-century customs house, this is one of the most atmospheric among Turin's hotels. It is small and has just 50 wood-pannelled rooms full of baroque furniture and furnishings. It is rumoured that Mozart and Verdi stayed here, but that was a long time ago...

C **Liberty**, via Pietro Micca 15, **T** 011 5628801, **F** 011 5622807, www.hotelliberty-torino.it *Map 2, D5, p252* On a road of fine art nouveau buildings, this palazzo is a fine example of liberty design. The 35 rooms are on the third floor and are furnished in tune with the architecture, with carpets on an original parquet floor. The rarefied atmosphere is said to attract an artsy, film-world clientele.

C **Victoria**, via Nino Costa 4, **T** 011 5611909, **F** 011 5611806 reservation@hotelvictoria-torino.com *Map 2, E8, p253* As the name suggests, this hotel is run by an anglophile and is kitted out in would-be Victorian that works in parts. The building itself actually dates from the1960s. All 106 of the rooms are decorated individually with English furnishings and touches, as seen through the Italian eye.

D **Amedeus e Teatro**, via Principe Amedeo 41/2, **T** 011 8174951. *Map 2, D9, p253* Right in the heart of bohemian via Po and university-land, this small hotel of 26 rooms has a charming, slightly Parisian atmosphere to match. It has no restaurant but breakfast is offered.

D **Best Western Genio**, C.so Vittorio Emanuele II 47/b, **T** 011 6505771, **F** 011 6508264, www.hotelgenio.it *Map 2, G9, p253* Chain-style modern rooms in a converted town house above the porticoes on Turin's main east-west drag. The rooms facing the street are rather noisy.

E **Des Artistes**, via Principe Amedeo 21/d, **T** 011 8124416. *Map 2, D9, p253* The name alone attracts would-be artists and the atmosphere here both in and around the hotel does not deceive or disappoint. Quiet and comfortable, this is one of Turin's best value and evocative addresses.

Lazy days
Strolling through the relaxed bohemian cobbled streets of the quadrilatero

F Casamarga bed & breakfast, via Bava 1/bis, **T** 011 883892.
Map 2, C11, p253 A little slice of family life near the river and in
prime studentland. Fun, noisy and cheap.

Le Langhe

There is really no excuse for not staying in an *agriturismo* amid
such lovely countryside, and the little villages between the main
wine towns offer many accommodation options visible from the
road. Accommodation in Albagets very booked up during the
festival season in October.

Alba

E **La Meridiana**, localita Altavilla 9, **T** 0173 440112 , no credit cards. A little outside town but therefore amid the rolling green hills. Six rooms in a liberty-style *casa padronale*. Very comfortable and clean with style and atmosphere.

F **Leon d'Oro**, piazza Marconi 2, **T** 0173 441901, **F** 0173 441901. Modern, clean yet an unspectacular option, centrally placed with 15 simple rooms, some with ensuite bath or shower.

F **Rovej**, via Silvio Pellico 18, **T** 0173 284306. A small and friendly guesthouse but with rather plain furnishings. Clean and functional.

The following *agriturismos* offer wine-tastings on site:

D **Erbaluna**, borgata Pozzo 43, **T** 0173 50800. En route from Alba to La Morra, this is a beautifully restored farmhouse with spacious, well-appointed rooms and period furniture in an isolated setting.

D **Villa la Favorita**, localia Altavilla 12/13, **T** 01733 64746, all cards accepted. About a mile from Alba, this is a turn of the century building, beautifully restored, clean and surrounded by vineyards with four double rooms.

Barolo

C **Hotel Barolo**, via Lomondo 2, **T** 0173 55191, **F** 0173 560026 www.hotelbarolo.it   Renowned yet stiff and establishment, known both for its accommodation and food.

E Fenocchio, via Alba 79, **T** 0173 560016. In Barolo, a disappointingly modern agriturismo offering wine- tastings in a fine rural setting in the heart of the region.

Asti

Rooms should be booked well in advance for the Palio horserace in September but otherwise finding accommodation is not a problem in Asti.

C Reale, piazza Alfieri 6, **T** 0141 530240, **F** 0141 34357, most cards accepted. Twenty-three rooms of fairly bland comfort but right in the centre of town.

D La Casa in Collina, localita Sant'Antonio 30, **T** 0141 822827, **F** 0141 823543. By far the best option, especially if you have a car. Beautifuly positioned on the hillside out of town and with six rooms offering romantic, spacious comfort.

E Cavour, piazza Marconi, **T** 0141 530222. A small modern and comfortable hotel and a decent cheap option.

E Genova, C.so Alessandria 26, **T** 0141 593197. Small, bright and reasonably homely hotel.

Susa

C Napoleon, via Mazzini 44, **T** 0122 622855. **F** 0122 31900. Hardly imperial but clean, comfortable, friendly and central.

D Il Mulino, localita Giordani 52, **T** 0122 238132. **F** 0122 38132. Agriturismo charm in a rambling and hospitable tumbling country farmhouse.

Saluzzo

D Le Camelie, via Collina 4, **T** 0175 85422. An agriturismo set amid lush, forested slopes within view of the Castello di Manta. Every effort should be made to stay here.

E Luna, via Martiri della Liberazione 10, **T** 0175 43707. A rustic take on modern furnishings situated within the medieval centre.

E Persico, vicolo Mercati, **T** 0175 41213. A small homely establishment tucked down a little medieval alleyway.

The Val d'Aosta

Aosta

Accommodation in Aosta is often expensive and fully booked as there is rarely a low season.

D La Belle Epoque, via d'Avise 18, **T** 0165 262276. Comprising a hotel and pizzeria, rooms here are modern, clean and comfortable if a little overpriced.

E Mochettaz, C.so Ivrea 107, **T** 0165 43706. Similarly functional and clean.

F La Ferme, regione Chabloz 18, **T** 0165 551647. An agriturismo offering farm-like accommodation on the outskirts of town in rural surroundings. Delicious homemade food.

F Milleluci T 0165 235278. A hotel-cum campsite in nearby Roppoz. Family-run and recently refurbished, it offers a cosy environment with clean simple rooms and good value tasty meals.

Ivrea

C **Aquila Antica**, via Gozzano 37, **T** 0125 641364, closed Sun, all cards accepted. Better known as a restaurant, see p164, but comfortable and convenient if you don't want far to go after a delicious meal.

D **Agriturismo La Miniera**, via Miniere 9, Lessolo, **T** 0125 58618. Not exactly convenient unless you have a car, this is a beautiful villa in the countryside.

E **Eden**, C.so d'Azeglio 67, **T** 0125 49190, **F** 0125 641293, www.mediturhotels.it A medium to large hotel offering bland chain comfort and all mod cons.

Campsites and cheaper hostels abound in the outlying villages and towns but for more precise information contact the Aosta tourist information office, see p30.

Time flies

Turin chimes with echoes of Italy's regal past, like this ornate clock in the Stupinigi hunting lodge.

Turin is bursting with high-quality restaurants ready to bombard you with local specialities that you may be unaware of and which form just as important a piece of the cultural jigsaw of the city and region as any museum. Meat and cheese are high on the agenda, which will please followers of Dr Atkins, although he would certainly not approve of the free-flowing Barolo wine.

Establishments vary from formal restaurants with all-too-attentive service and a rarified atmosphere to friendly, rough-and-tumble trattorias, osterias and pizzerias. Attention is firmly focused on the flavour of the food and rarely on trendy concept decors where the design bill is included in the menu prices. Most establishments listed below are in fact rather plain places where greater attention is paid to fine nuances and combinations in flavour. Turin's eateries tend to be warm, traditional places where a three-course meal with wine still remains incredibly good value.

€ **Eating codes**

€€€   45 and over
€€   25-45
€   25 and under

Prices are per head for a three course meal (antipasto, secondo and dolce) excluding wine.

Make sure you try some of the out-of-town recommendations as these restaurants are very often in superb rural locations and even closer to the origins and true flavours of the always locally produced ingredients. Ethnic cuisine is taken seriously and not just for late-night munchies or drinking fodder. Any ethnic restaurant that survives in Italy is worth a look for good food and a change of scene. It is also worth bearing in mind that since the Italians never like to be too far from food, and will take great care over its preparation in all circumstances, you can also get decent food in many of the bars and cafés, often until late into the night (see p165).

Practical information

Turin's better restaurants tend to be very booked up, especially at weekends. Restaurant opening hours are regimented: lunch is served 1230-1500 with kitchens closing promptly. In the evening most restaurants open at around 1930-2000 and the kitchens close at around 2300 with osterie and café-restaurants staying open until 0100. Beware of days when your favourite or planned restaurant might be closed: it tends to be on a Monday or Tuesday evening, or for half a day on either of those days; pizzerias do not close on Mondays, however. Real osterias and trattorias (as opposed to those who use the name for false authenticity) work more rural hours and are not usually open for lunch. Visitors in August are also liable to be disappointed as many restaurants, if not the whole of metropolitan Italy, close for most of the month, especially the middle two weeks.

Price

Eating and drinking

Credit cards are increasingly accepted but in cheaper restaurants, osterias and trattorias, only cash will be accepted.

Specialities

Surprisingly to many visitors, Turin is the source of a number of the most-exported and stereotypical elements of Italian cuisine. For a start there are those long thin sticks of bread in plastic wrappers that you nibble on either while waiting to order or instead of a starter. *Grissini* have been a speciality of Turin's cuisine since the 17th century (see box, p142). But before that you might have had an aperitif of either Vermouth or Martini, both locally brewed drinks.

Primi piatti (starters)

To start with you might like to try some of the local cold meats like the *salama d'la duja* (a lardy type of salami sausage), or *salame d'oca* (goose meat) from Novara, mixed with some of the well known local cheeses such as soft *Toma*, tangy *Bra* made from a mix of cow's and ewe's milk or *Castelmagno*, so-called as it was a favourite of Charlemagne. On the side, you might want a few *asparagi* (asparagus sticks) from Santena, *carciofi ripieni* (stuffed artichokes) or onions from Ivrea, or *pepperoni*, baked and peeled peppers marinated in an anchovy sauce from Asti. *Le acciughe* (anchovies) are big in Turin and form the basis for one of the staples of local peasant food, the *bagna cauda*, a garlicky stew of vegetables including peppers, radishes and onions mixed with anchovy. Other local primi piatti to try are *gnocchi alla bava* (potato dumplings with cheese) and some of the risotto dishes, as nearby Vercelli on the plain between Turin and Milan is the rice capital of Europe. Anything which says *alle trofie bianche* (with white truffles) is unmissable although liable to be expensive; you won't regret it though if you're a truffle fan. Piemonte is not as big on pasta as, say, Emilia Romagna, but the two specialities here are *agnolotti* (like ravioli with spinach stuffing) and *tajarin*, a thin tagliatelle.

I drink therefore I am

Masquerade as one of Turin's literary and political elite in one of the beautifully restored period cafés

> ### The origins of grissini

In 1684, Vittorio Amedeo, the nine-year-old heir to the Savoy throne, was ill. The doctor said he needed a light type of bread to digest and so the then royal cook, Antonio Brunero, invented the grissino. Slowly nibbling away on the bread sticks, the young heir recovered and when he took over as Duke of Savoy he celebrated the value of this type of daily bread.

So the grissini passed from royal medicine and trend into Italian gastronomy, doubly revered since it lasts much longer than bread itself. The name derives from the word 'grisse' or 'gherssa', a type of bread fashionable in the 18th century. In theory, it should be eaten with prosciutto twirled around it or crumbled over an antipasto.

Secondi (main courses)

The heavyweights of Piemontese cuisine are veal dishes, especially the *brasato al Barolo* (brazed in a Barolo sauce) or *tonné all'italienne* (a light creamy tuna based sauce). More basic and like a Hungarian goulash is the *bollito misto*, a stew of all parts of many animals that is very tasty despite thoughts of the details. The nearby rivers also provide ample *trota* (trout) and *carpa* (carp) which provide a refreshing alternative to the potential meat overdose.

Dolci (desserts)

There is always room for pudding and Turin must have Italy's sweetest tooth. Among the smooth naughty delights to savour are the *zabaglione*, *panna cotta* (crème brulée) and all manner of *torroni* (chocolate cakes) made from almond and other variants on the theme of the famous torinese creamy dark chocolate called *gianduja*. Finish off with a cup of espresso coffee, very likely to be made from Lavazza coffee – the Turin-based company that invented the first Italian coffee machine.

Wine

Forget your Chianti and Lambrusco, Turin is the Italian capital of wine with the king of reds, Barolo, and his dukes, the Barbaresco, Barbera and Nebbiolo, all being made just a few miles away. Don't miss also the friendly and very quaffable of a country lunchtime Dolcetto, and the Roero. If you want bubbles, the much maligned Asti Spumante and Moscato del Monferrato are unrecognizable in comparison to the bottles found in British supermarkets.

Centre

Cafés

Caffe San Carlo, piazza San Carlo 156. *Open all day until 0100. Map 2, E6, p252* More like a museum, this grand café with its internal Corinthian columns and sculptures and paintings that could grace a royal court is the centerpiece of Turin's café life. Unmissable for its regal atmosphere.

Caffe Torino, piazza San Carlo 204. *Open all day until 0100. Map 2, E7, p253* The main rival to *Caffe San Carlo* and equally over the top in its twirly decadent decor. Torino was historically the haunt of visiting Hollywood stars.

Confetteria Baratti, Galleria Subalpina. *Open all day until 0100. Map 2, D7, p253* A historic cornerstone of Turin's intellectual past, this is a gloriously decadent café under the arcades of piazza Castello, with a marble bar and tables, wood-panelling and mirrors. It is famous for its pastries and the house cocktail, *CioCio San*, named after the character from the opera *Madam Butterfly*. A favourite of the poet, Guido Gozzano.

▶ **The capital of *cioccolato***

Chocolate arrived in Italy through its links with Spain. The Aztecs had discovered or invented 'xocolatl', a drink they referred to as a drink of the Gods. Chocolate arrived in Europe through the Spanish conquistadors, and with the marriage in 1587 of Carlo Emanuele I, son of Duke Emanuele Filiberto I, to Caterina, daughter of Felipe II of Spain, it passed into Italy as a rarefied royal tipple. The people of Italy had to wait until 1678 for the Savoys to grant permission to Giovambattista Ari to repro-duce the art of chocolate manufacture in Italy, and ever since then Turin has been the capital of Italian chocolate. The symbol of this saccharine supremacy is the *gianduiotto*, first made for the 1867 carnival and invented by the chocolatiers *Prochet & Gay* who pioneered the thick creamy mix of cacao with nocciola and named their invention after the torinese carnival mask, the *Gianduja*.

Confetteria Stratta, piazza San Carlo 191. *Map 2, E7, p253* Famous for its *crema gianduja* chocolate and other delicious and naughty fondants (thick, hot and sweet drinks).

San Tommaso 10 – Ristorante Lavazza, via San Tommaso 10. *Open all day until 0100. Map 2, D5, p252 Starbucks* eat your heart out: here, from the home of Lavazza coffee, are all the types and preparations you could want. Try the fruits of the forest espresso and a solid espresso! There's a good restaurant here, too, and the history of Lavazza advertising is plastered all over the walls.

Restaurants

€ € € **El Centenario**, via Biancamano 3, **T** 011 539506. *Map 2, F5, p252* Tortilla, nachos and the best of the rest of Mexico on a plate in a good quality restaurant. A spicy and sunny change from the Italian staples.

€€€ **'L Gentilom**, via Gobetti 15, **T** 011 5577111. *Map 2, F7, p253* Set within the stylish *Hotel Principi di Piemonte,* this is an appropriately smart, if a little formal and quiet restaurant. If you're staying here you'll probably want to eat out; not many locals come here just for the food.

€€€ **Mister Hu**, via Mercanti 16, **T** 011 537171. *Map 2, D5, p252* Offering a vast menu across the regions of China, this is considered to be Turin's best Chinese restaurant.

€€€ **Neuv Caval 'd Brons**, piazza San Carlo, **T** 011 5627483. *Map 2, E7, p253* Set in Turin's showcase piazza, this is one of the city's gastronomic classics. The menu has kept up with the times offering an innovative and sometimes surprising take on traditional regional dishes.

€€ **La Smarrita**, via Cesare Battisti 17, **T** 011 8177679. *Map 2, D7, p253* This restaurant is supposed to be located in the former offices of Cavour, the founder of the Italian consitution. This piece of history has nothing to do with the menu other than ensure pride in delicious local specialities.

€ **Arcadia**, Galleria Subalpina 16, **T** 011 561 3898. *Map 2, D6, p252* Sushi meets Piemontese cuisine in this bar/restaurant that's not so much fusion as bilingual, with your *tempura* and *udon* served at the bar and traditional regional dishes at the surrounding tables.

€ **Barattino**, piazza Castello 27, **T** 011 5613060. *Map 2, D7, p253* This is the restaurant off-shoot of the famous *Baratti café*. Perfectionists might say they should stick to their main business but the cuisine is flavoursome and local, and the decor traditional and elegant in the stylish core of the city.

Northeast and Borgo Po

Cafés

Dezzutto, via Duchessa Jolanda 23/b. *Open all day until 2300. Map 1, F3, p250* A 1950s style haven and a favourite for sweet-toothed journalists.

Caffe Fiorio, via Po 8. *Open all day until 0100. Map 2, D8, p253* Famous for being the favourite of Cavour, d'Azeglio and others of Italy's founding fathers, Fiorio was where the latest political news and views began and spread.

Restaurants

€ € € **La Barrique**, C.so Dante 53/a, **T** 011 657900. *Map 3, F9, p255* A refined and formal atmosphere greets customers at this, one of Turin's classiest dining rooms, serving exquisite regional dishes like a cream of artichoke and peppers starter and tagliatelle.

€ € € **Caffe Elena**, via Matteo Pescatore 9, **T** 011 837760. *Map 2, D11, p253* Currently one of Turin's cooler hang-outs, more for its trendy minimalism, lounge music and general bar scene than for its food however, it is nevertheless beautifully prepared and presented and very tasty.

€ € € **Mare Nostrum**, via Matteo Pescatore 16, **T** 011 8394543. *Map 2, D11, p253* A local bastion of seafood cuisine, delicious but at a price.

⭐ **Best**

Restaurants

- Combal.Zero – for nouvelle cuisine in a castle setting, p160
- Del Cambio – for gourmets and history, p150
- Gennaro Esposito – for the best pizza in town, p155
- Tre Galline – for quantity and quality, p154
- Valenza – for humble working-class origins, p159

€€ **Al 24**, via Montebello 24, **T** 011 8122981. *Map 2, C9, p253*
Another lively and good-value eatery around the Mole
Antonelliana mixing Piemontese and Tuscan cuisine with plenty of
truffle dishes when in season.

€€ **Al Fortin**, via Damiano Chiesa 8, **T** 011 2731672. *Map 1, A6,
p250* With ingredients all locally-sourced and fresh, the
Piemontese dishes served here are very full flavoured.

€€ **Cave du Jour**, C.so San Maurizio 69, **T** 011 836145, *closed
Sun, only open in evenings, all cards except Amex. Map 2, B10, p253*
Near arcaded piazza Vittorio, this recently opened restaurant with
vaulted, bare-brick ceilings projects a traditional and simple
atmosphere. The extensive wine list makes it more of a winery-
cum-restaurant and in summer it is nice just to sit at the outside
tables and sample a glass or two. The menu offers a wide range of
wholesome taverna-style dishes.

€€ **Finestre sul Po**, Lungo Po Cadorna 1, **T** 011 8123633. *Map 2,
D12, p253* Set on the left bank of the languorous river Po but not
really with a view, you will probably want to concentrate on the
delicious food served here anyway, in particular the risotto.

€€ **La Cloche**, strada Traforo del Pino 106, **T** 011 8994213. *Map 1,
A8, p250* A cosy family run restaurant set across the river and

therefore a little out of the way, specializing in a game-oriented menu of rich regional dishes.

€€ **Monferrato**, via Monferrato 6, **T** 011 8190661. *Map 2, D13, p253* A real slice of Piemonte from the food down to the dialect of the waiters and chef. All the local favourites are on offer here in genuine local surroundings.

€€ **Porto di Savona**, piazza Vittorio Veneto 2, **T** 011 8173500. *Map 2, D11, p253* Under the arcades looking out over piazza Vittorio, this traditional restaurant serves regional dishes with a slant towards the rice-based cuisine of the Novara region.

€ **Le Otto Colonne**, via Giulia di Barolo 5, **T** 011 836507. *Map 2, C11, p253* A mixture of dishes from both Piemonte and the Abruzzi region in Turin's studenty neighbourhood.

€ **Paglia e Fieno Bistrot**, C.so Fiume 11/a, **T** 011 6604036. *Map 2, G12, p253* More of a French restaurant serving both Italian and French staples, often to the accompaniment of live music and therefore open late.

€ **Pizzeria Caffe del Progresso**, C.so San Maurizio 69/b, **T** 011 837914. *Lunch only. Map 2, B10, p253* With its name, this ace pizzeria announces its politico-intellectual ambitions, harking back to the revolutionary years of the 1920s and 1930s. Alongside the food, there are often literature recitals and live music.

€ **Pizzeria Cristina**, C.so Palermo, **T** 011 2481706. *Map 1, C5, p250* The best pizza in the northeast of the city, served up in typically no-nonsense pizzeria surroundings.

€ **Sotto la Mole**, via Montebello 9, **T** 011 8179398, *closed Wed, only open evenings, most cards accepted. Map 2, C9, p253*

As the name says, right under the Mole and therefore in prime lively studentland, a bustling restaurant with great meat and pasta dishes.

€ **Zero Pizza**, via Luigi Tarino 3, **T** 011 8129743. *Map 2, B10, p253* A shrine to Italian muso Renato Zero – on the music system, in the photos and in the clothes he wore on stage, also displayed. Every pizza is even named after a Zero song. If you don't recognize the music you haven't missed anything, but Zero is a pillar of that particular type of Italian music.

Southeast

Cafés

Café-Gelateria Pepino, piazza Carignano 8. *Open all day until 2300. Map 2, D7, p253* Established over 100 years ago, this should be your first port of call for a torinese ice cream.

Caffe Platti, C.so Vittorio Emanuele II 72. *Open all day until 0100. Map 2, G6, p252* Away from the baroque of *Café San Carlo*, Platti evokes more the style of Louis XVI with its lighter, more effeminate pastel shades. This is where Juventus was born and where the poet Cesare Pavese liked to drink, so you will be in good company.

Restaurants

€ € € **Al Garamond**, via Pomba 14, **T** 011 8122781. *Map 2, F8, p253* Delicious antipasti are the speciality in this traditional restaurant, among them the goats cheese ravioli. Also don't miss the quail in truffle sauce and the original liquorice mousse.

€ € € **Carignano**, via Carlo Alberto 35, **T** 011 5170171. *Map 2, E8, p253* Different from many of the city's other hotel restaurants, this one set in the *Grand Hotel Sitea* is a chic and classy dining room with a deservedly chic and therefore formal clientele. Good for a romantic evening but low on lively atmosphere.

€€€ **Ristorante del Cambio**, piazza Carignano 2, **T** 011 543760. *Map 2, D7, p253* Marinated in a long-standing aristocratic tradition, this restaurant, open since 1757, is one of Turin's most illustrious. The decor is operatic with abundant mirrors, stucco and frescoes; the food and service very much in the same style. The long list of illustrious diners includes Cavour, the architect of the Italian State; the management have managed to remember where he sat all those years ago so you can follow in his footsteps.

€€€ **San Giorgio 1884**, viale Millo 6, **T** 011 6692131. *Map 3, E12, p255* Set within the facsimile medieval village, what might be a rather gimmicky establishment is in fact quite tasteful. Founded in 1884, the walls are frescoed and the furnishings antique while the menu is international to suit the palates of the main visitors, tourists. Sometime there is live music and most nights there is a piano bar.

€€€ **Torpedo**, via Nizza 262, **T** 011 6642000. *Map 1, J6, p251* As part of the refurbished, super-contemporary Lingotto complex, this restaurant in the *Meridien Lingotto* hotel is suitably minimalist and contemporary – one of only a few in Turin – and the dishes sometimes a little too much so.

€€ **L'Agrifoglio**, via Accademia Albertina 38/d, **T** 011 4366706/ 837064, closed Sun and Mon, only open in evenings, most cards accepted. *Map 2, F8, p253* Delicious and good-value homemade cooking in heart of stylish baroque Turin. If you like risotto, try the rice with *crema Barbaresco* sauce. The puddings are unavoidable.

€€ **Hosteria la Vallee**, via Provana 3/b, **T** 011 8121788. *Map 2, F10, p253* As the name suggests this is a down-at-heel tavern-style eaterie, more than a little influenced by France, notably in the delicious foie gras starters.

€€ **Montecarlo**, via San Francesco da Paola 37, **T** 011 888763. *Map 2, E8, p253* Delicious dishes from all over northern Italy in a friendly, cosmopolitan atmosphere.

€€ **Spada Reale**, via Principe Amedeo 53, **T** 011 8171363. *Map 2, D8, p253* If you've never eaten bison, now's your chance; if you've got any room left try the risotto and the orange mousse.

€ **Da Angelino**, C.so Moncalieri 59, **T** 011 6602267. *Map 3, A12, p255* A family run atmosphere in a friendly restaurant which specializes in regional, in particular game, cuisine. Allegedly a favourite with local celebs and footballers.

€ **Dai Saletta**, via Belfiore 37, no phone, closed Sun, all cards accepted. *Map 3, B8, p255* Checkcloth-decorated and family run, this is a typical warm and intimate restaurant in two small rooms with superb homemade local classics such as tripe, truffle ravioli and *brasato al Barolo*.

€ **Estrela do Sul**, via Nizza 23, **T** 011 6699472. *Map 2, H7, p253* Should you have the urge to eat Brazilian food, or simply sample a Brazilian atmosphere among Turin's significant population of *brazileros*, this is the place.

€ **Kirkuk Café**, via Carlo Alberto 16/b, **T** 011 530657. *Map 2, F8, p253* If you've never had a chance to taste Kurdish cuisine, why not start here? Superior falafels and delicious aubergine and other vegetable dishes in the Greek-Mediterranean mould.

€ **L'Idrovolante**, viale Virgilio 105, **T** 011 6687602. *Map 2, H11, p253* Set within the parco Valentino this romantic restaurant is

⭐ **Best**

Cafés

• Al Bicerin – for delicious and cosy tradition, p156
• Caffe Elena – for a lively bohemian cappuccino, p146
• Caffe San Carlo – for the sophistication of past times, p143
• Caffe Torino – for original belle époque elegance, p143
• Divan Café – for literary inspiration, p156

decorated with mosaic tiles more reminiscent of Spain or Portugal, while picture windows afford lovely panoramic views. The menu does not disappoint and the *gnocchetti di castagne* (little chestnut dumplings) in red wine should not be missed.

€ **Imbarco Perosino da Graziella**, viale Virglio 53, **T** 011 657362. *Map 2, H11, p253* In the parco Valentino behind the regal architecture faculty building, this restaurant is over 100 years old, with great renditions of local themes such as *antipasti di flan*, *bagna cauda* and veal in a nut sauce.

€ **La Scaletta**, via Giuria 27/d, **T** 011 655763. *Map 3, D10, p255* A great place for truffle lovers, the dumplings stuffed with truffle sauce are exquisite while the mains and substantial sweet trolley are equally irresistible.

€ **Le Vitel Etonne**, via San Francesco de Paola 4, **T** 011 8124621. *Map 2, E9, p253* More of a winery than a restaurant but the food served up is delicious and substantial – it's just a question of priorities and the rustic atmosphere emphasizes this. Meaning 'the surprised calf', most of it seems to have ended up on the menu.

€ **Spaccanapoli**, via Mazzini 19, **T** 011 8126694. *Map 2, G8, p253* Genuine Neapolitan piazzas and in genuine Neapolitan company, this is a simple and fun place for a snack or light meal.

Southwest

Cafés

Ornato di Te, via Ornato 4. *Map 2, C13, p253* A detox, non- alcoholic café-bar, very green and eco-friendly.

Restaurants

€ € € **Al Gatto Nero**, C.so Turati 14, **T** 011 590477. *Map 2, E6, p252* For those who like Tuscan dishes this is the place to come. Especially great soups and fish dishes.

€ € € **Il Porticciolo**, via Barletta 58, **T** 011 321601. *Map 1, I3, p251* Really exquisite seafood and other dishes prepared in ways and with sauces the like of which you won't have eaten before. The artichokes in champagne are particularly unmissable.

€ € € **Marco Polo**, via Marco Polo 38, **T** 011 500096. *Map 3, D2, p254* Turin is not by the sea, but the fish arrives daily fresh from Genoa and the Ligurian coast. Testament to this is the amazing array of fish and other seafood dishes on offer here.

€ € € **Moreno**, C.so Unione Sovietica 244, **T** 011 3179657. *Map 1, I5, p251* A short trek halfway down one of Turin's seemingly endless arterial boulevards, formerly called the *Prima Smarrita*, this restaurant still has the same chef who specializes in menu of fish and meat dishes in accordance with the seasons.

€ € € **Trait d'Union**, via Stampatori 4, **T** 011 5612506. *Map 2, E4, p252* A good reference point for the vegetarian in what is otherwise a carnivore's paradise, this restaurant serves tasty dishes from all over Italy, also some with meat.

€€€ **Vigna Reale**, via Sacchi 8, **T** 011 5625511. *Map 2, H6, p252* Set within the exclusive atmosphere of the *Turin Palace Hotel*, the food here is good but pricey and you risk dining with your fellow tourists.

€€€ **Vintage 1997**, piazza Solferino 16/h, **T** 011 535948. *Map 2, F5, p252* A selection of dishes from all over Italy are offered in refined surroundings, more contemporary and therefore less stuffy than many of Turin's establishments.

€€ **Il 58**, via San Secondo 58, **T** 011 505566. *Map 3 , B6, p254* More of a Parisian bistro than a restaurant, specializing in a wide range of seafood dishes.

€€ **Le Tre Galline**, via Bellezia 37, **T** 011 4366553. *Map 2, D4, p252* One of the oldest and most famous addresses in Turin's gastronomic landscape, with over 300 years of tradition under the ever-expanding belt of its owners. Far from labouring under its reputation, the restaurant still serves immaculate and sumptuous local dishes at a price tag that could be much worse.

€€ **Nuovo Ristorante Crocetta**, via Marco Polo 21, **T** 011 597789. *Map 3, D2, p254* A modern restaurant near one of Turin's main fruit and vegetable markets serving a contemporary take on dishes from all over Italy and a wide-reaching wine list to match.

€€ **Osteria Antiche Sere**, via Cenischia 9, **T** 011 3854347, *closed Sun, only open in evenings, no cards accepted. Map 1, G3, p251* Stuck down a narrow alley of this former working-class district, this osteria retains its honest decor and atmosphere and serves delicious homemade regional dishes in three cosy rooms and outside.

€€ **Taverna dei Guitti**, via San Dalmazzo 1, **T** 011 533164, *closed Sat lunch and all Sun*, most cards accepted. *Map 2, D4, p252*

In the heart of 18th-century Turin, this homely tavern is dedicated to musical and theatrical shows while you eat. An intimate and flavoursome gastro-artistic experience that is recommended.

€ € **Villa Somis**, strada Val Pattonera 138, **T** 011 6613086. *Map1, F8, p251* A high-class alternative to the regional fare which can be heavy and overly rich at times, Somis offers a lighter more typically Mediterranean menu, with the according options of fish.

€ **C'era Una Volta**, C.so Vittorio Emanuele II 41, **T** 011 6504589. *Map 2, H3, p252* Robust local fare in a classic setting under the arcades of the city's central boulevards. A great place to try the *bagna cauda* and *fonduta* dishes, washed down with solid red wine.

€ **Gennaro Esposito**, via Passalacqua 1/g, **T** 011 535905. *Map 2 E1, p252* A classic Neapolitan name for a classic Neapolitan establishment serving fine examples of that city's famous export – the pizza – both crisp and slightly sloppy like they're supposed to be and no fancy toppings, just the old favourites.

€ **L'Angolo Greco**, C.so Vittorio Emanuele II 40, **T** 011 888855. *Map 2, H3, p252* As the name implies, a corner of Greece in Turin, but don't think dodgy kebabs and retsina, the food here does justice to a cuisine that was one of the great contributors to what we now know as Italian food.

€ **Solferino**, piazza Solferino 3, **T** 011 535851. *Map 2, E5, p252* A marriage of Tuscan and Piemontese dishes for the discerning gastronome, all served strictly according to seasonal and local availability of the ingredients.

€ **Wasabi**, C.so Ferrucci 75, **T** 011 4473812. *Map 1, F3, p250* A tasty but not over atmospheric corner of Japan, good to quell any sudden and irrepressible sushi cravings.

€ **Whopee**, via Boucheron 17/c, **T** 011 541808. *Map 2, D1, p252* A light-hearted and simple pizzeria perfect for a cheap and wholesome meal.

Northwest

Cafés

Al Bicerin, piazza della Consolata 5. *Open all day until 2230. Map 2, B3, p252* If you go to one café in Turin it should be this one, even if it has become a tourist favourite of late. Tiny, cosy, smoky and Parisian, and with all its original wood furnishings, this café will inspire you to write poetry even if you didn't know you had it in you. This is where Silvio Pellico sat and wrote *Le mie Prigioni* on his release from the Spielberg jail. Al Bicerin is also famous for the 'bicerin'– a delicious, thick mixture of coffee, chocolate and cream, also with a hint of grappa if you like, perfect for a foggy winter's afternoon.

Al Caffe Molassi, via Borgo Dora 23, **T** 0339 6918087. *Open 1900-2300. Map 2, A4, p252* A genuine tavern with robust regional meals and wines, great crepes and *frullati* (milkshakes).

Divan Café, via Baretti 15/c, **T** 011 6698049. *Open all day until 2300. Map 3, A9, p255* Full of books for reading with a drink or for sale, this is an intellectual café-bar in the heart of a multi- ethnic district of Turin.

Fusion Café, via Sant'Agostino 17/f, **T** 011 4365022. *Open all day until 0100. Map 2, C4, p252* Similar in decor to *Hafa café*, this mellow café has private cubby holes for added intimacy.

Hafa Café, via Sant'Agostino 23/c. *Open all day until 0100. Map 2, C4, p252* Styled like a cool white-washed Moroccan country house and hung with Morocciana – copper dishes, lattice wooden chairs and so on which are all for sale. Enjoy a mint tea, tisane or various alcoholic alternatives.

I Tre Galli, via Sant'Agostino 25, **T** 011 5216027. *Open 1930-2330. Map 2, C4, p252* In the heart of the *quadrilatero romano*, this is a fashionable restaurant for a glass of wine or for a fine regional meal, popular with a regular youthful clientele.

L'Obelix Café, piazza Savoia 4, **T** 011 4367206. *Open 1930-0200. Map 2, C3, p252* Two floors connected by a fluorescent futuristic staircase, and covered in collages based on old cinema posters. Arty, trendy and popular for aperitifs and light meals.

Osteria del Balon, via Borgo Dora **T** 011 4368755. *Open 1900-2300. Map 2, A4, p252* Good old-fashioned tradition with homemade ingredients and a strong selection of regional wines in an honest working-class setting.

Sapor Divino, via Borgo Dora 35, **T** 011 4365104. *Open 1900-2330. Map 2, A4, p252* As the name states, a bar/restaurant dedicated to the taste buds. Wine and regional dish tastings are held in a cosy, informal setting.

Tisaneria della Consolata, via della Consolata 2. *Open all day until 2200. Map 2, B3, p252* Detox bar offering every tisane under the sun, including several homemade concoctions. Served up to relaxing tunes with a mellow vibe.

Restaurants

€€€ **La Marquiserie**, via Giulio 4, **T** 011 4361396. *Map 2, B3, p252* Specializes in seafood. Even if you're not normally a fan it's worth trying the house specialities which have a Tuscan slant.

★ Aperitif bars

- Hafa Café, p156
- Fusion Café, p156
- L'Aperitivo, p168
- La Drogheria, p168
- Luce e Gas, p175

€€€ **Savoia**, via Corte d'Appello 13, **T** 011 4362288. *Map 2, C4, p252* Despite its name, this restaurant serves up interesting and tasty eastern-fusion takes on typical Italian dishes, although octopus in tempura recalls Japan more readily than Italy.

€€ **L'Osto del Borgh Vej**, via Torquato Tasso 7, **T** 011 4364843. *Map 2, C5, p252* Another of Turin's old favourites with the popular touch. A great place to try the Piemontese speciality, *vitello tonnato* (veal in a tomato-based sauce).

€ **Antica Bruschetteria Pautasso**, piazza E. Filliberto 4, **T** 011 4366706. *Map 2, B4, p252* A good place to enjoy the honest local favourites such as *bagna cauda* in a simple but characterful setting.

€ **Osteria il Tagliere**, piazza E. Filiberto 3/b **T** 011 5217882. *Map 2, B4, p252* An olde-worlde tavern/restaurant proudly serving regional and folky dishes with the emphasis on the homemade as well as a long menu of over 50 locally produced alpine cheeses.

€ **San Giors**, via Borgo Dora, **T** 011 5211256. *Map 2, A4, p252* Despite the new management and refurbishment this, one of Turin's oldest restaurants, still delights with a menu steeped in the experience and full flavour of 300 years of regional cooking.

€ **Stars and Roses**, piazza Paleocapa 2, **T** 011 5162052. *Map 2, G6, p252* A simple but tasty pizzeria, popular on Sunday evenings, and serving the full range of classic toppings.

€ **Valenza**, via Borgo Dora 39, **T** 011 5213914. *Map 2, A4, p252* If one restaurant should drag you to this regenerated working-class area by night, it should be Valenza, where the wood-panelling and humble, rustic atmosphere on top of the food are a delight and recall a previous era.

Around Turin

In the hills around Turin above Borgo Nuovo

€€€ **Locanda Mongreno**, strada Mongreno 50, **T** 011 8980417. A romantic, low-light setting in which to enjoy local cuisine reinvented with the odd innovative touch from the house chef.

€ **Birilli**, strada Val San Martino 6, **T** 011 8190567. Currently a very trendy out-of-town restaurant with a good atmosphere and an innovative take on traditional regional recipes.

€ **Pavia**, viale Thovez 60/b, **T** 011 6602060. A visual as well as gastronomic feast, containing an amazing array of colours, shapes and tastes along with a spread of some 50 antipasti dishes on the buffet.

€ **Trattoria con Calma**, strada Comunale del Cartman, **T** 011 8980229. Intimate and cosy by a log fire in winter and airy and open in summer with tables outside. A friendly, relaxed and tasty option away from the centre.

€ **Trattoria Decoratori e Imbianchini**, via Lanfanchi 278, **T** 011 8190672. A traditional taverna-type eatery, historically visited by painters (the decorator type, not Leonardo), situated within a garden where tables are placed in the summer months. A relaxing place in which to enjoy robust local cuisine.

€ **Trattoria della Posta**, strada Mongreno 16, **T** 011 8980193. A place of pilgrimage for cheese lovers, for every type of local cheese is on offer along with other regional dishes in a friendly rural and humble setting.

Near the castles on the outskirts of Turin

€€€ **Combal.Zero**, piazza Mafalda di Savoia, Rivoli, **T** 011 9565225. Set within Rivoli castle, this restaurant is as contemporary and challenging as the art in the museum next door, including the speciality 'cyberegg' – an eggshell filled with caviar and vodka, drunk in one go like a shot. Very charismatic, classy and tasty.

€€€ **Maison Delfino**, via Lagrange 4, Moncalieri, **T** 011 642552. In the heart of the exclusive centre of Moncalieri, near the castle, this is a pricey but stylish venue serving a broad range of regional and Italian meat and seafood dishes.

€€ **Il Reale**, C.so Garibaldi 153, Veneria Reale, **T** 011 4530413. Royal food in a royal setting near the Mandria castle and grounds.

€ **Sabaudia**, viale Torino 11, Stupinigi, **T** 011 3580119. More about the setting than the menu (which doesn't disappoint), this restaurant in the Stupinigi grounds is set within the decorative walls of the Savoy's extravagant dreams. Live and eat like a duke for a night.

Alba

Café-bars

Good bars where it is possible to taste wines with snacks are:

Enoteca Fracchia, via Vernazza 29. An olde-worlde wine bar serving delicious meat and cheese snacks and offering varied wine tasting.

'L Crotin, via Cuneo 3. A small bar-restaurant serving rustic portions of regional food.

Vincafé, via Vittorio Emanuele 12. A trendy and café-cum-wine bar popular around aperitif time.

Restaurants

€€ **Enoclub**, piazza Savona 2, **T** 0173 33994. *Closed Mon.* A winery and restaurant serving delicious Langhe food on Alba's most vibrant piazza, ideal for an aperitif at passeggiata time or for a slap-up meal downstairs.

€€ **Lalibera**, via Pertinace 24a, **T** 0173 293155. *Closed all Sun and Mon lunch.* Makes a point of not serving truffles in October as there are allegedly many 'fakes' but the rest of the menu more than makes up for this.

€€ **Osteria dell'Arco**, piazza Savona 5, **T** 0173 363974. *Closed Sun all day and Mon lunch.* Great local dishes and a specialization in cheese dishes in a pretty setting in an arcaded courtyard of the square.

And for a nice dolce to finish the evening off, try **Io, Tu el dolci** on piazza Savona, a café/ice cream parlour.

Barolo

Restaurants

€€ **La Cantinella**, via Acquagelata 4a, **T** 0173 56267. *Closed Mon evenings and all Tues*. Renowned as one of the best trattorie in a region where you can't really go wrong.

€€ **Locanda della Posta di Barolo**, piazza Municipio 4/1, **T** 0173 56385. Equally wonderful flavours in a peaceful and genuine rural setting. Also sell their own wine.

Asti

Restaurants

€€ **Fratelli Rovero**, localita Valdonata, **T** 0141 530102. *Closed Sun eve and all Mon. No cards. I*t is worth the trip out to this agriturismo-restaurant 5 km out of town, serving sumptuous and plentiful dishes and specializing in a local menu.

€€ **Osteria ai Binari**, Frazione Mombarone 145, **T** 0141 294228. *All cards accepted.* Also some 5 km out of town, situated in a converted railway building. The food is delicious, the service friendly and the clientele young and vibrant.

€ **Trattoria Aurora**, viale Partigiana 58, closed Mon. Excellent local cuisine.

The Val de Susa

Restaurants

Susa has many small-time eateries and pizzerias.

€€ **Sant' Antonio di Susa**, **T** 011 9631747. *Closed Tues. All cards accepted.*   Near the Sacra di San Michele, this restaurant in the countryside is considered the best in the area. Worth booking ahead.

Saluzzo

Restaurants

€€ **L'Ostu dij Baloss**, via Gualtieri 38, **T** 0175 248618. *Closed Sun and also Mon lunch, all cards except Amex.*   An historic and delightful place to sample local wines and dishes in an amiable and nostalgically courteous environment.

The Val d'Aosta

Val d'Aosta food is robust alpine fare with specialities being polenta with sausages washed down with a rich red wine and followed by grappa. One thing you should definitely try out (and buy from the myriad craft shops) is a *grolla valdostana*, a wooden teapot with six or eight spouts, sometimes more . It contains Italian espresso coffee, a healthy dose of grappa and a touch of lemon or orange juice. Alcohol-laced sugar is sprayed liberally on top and then the brew is lit, like an English Christmas pudding. Once the flame dies out, the top is replaced and the assembled drink is poured from the spouts, and the grolla is passed around like a loving cup.

Aosta

In Aosta, the streets of via Aubert, via d'Anselmo and via Porta Pretoria are lined with smart restaurants.

Restaurants

€€€ **Trattoria degli Artisti**, via Maillet 5-7, **T** 0165 4096. A favourite among gourmet locals, specializing in delicious and robust local dishes.

€€ **La Cave**, via Challand 34, **T** 0165 44164. *0900-2100, closed Sun.* Rich local delicacies in one of the most renowned establishments in town.

Ivrea

Café-bars

Hopstore, via lago S Michele 13, **T** 0125 616195. Ivrea nightlife won't set the world on fire but this is one of the liveliest of the drinking holes on offer, also serving good snacks.

Restaurants

€€ **Aquila Antica**, via Gozzano 37, **T** 0125 641364. *Closed Sun, all cards accepted.* Open since 1976, this is a locally renowned address, particularly for its delicious hospitality.

Turin's stylish and buzzing café and nightlife scene is one of the most surprising aspects of a city famed for its industry, grey weather and dull personality. Turin's cafés have long been famous as the place where 19th-century Parisian-style intellectuals gathered, reflected and gave birth to such things as the Italian nation, political movements and great football teams over a lingering cappuccino. For the most historic hotspots, still with lavish Parisian interiors, head for piazza Castello and piazza San Carlo. Most cafés are suitably open well into the early hours and also offer a good range of smaller meals and snacks.

The revitalized *quadrilatero romano*, north of via Garibaldi, is virtually wall-to-wall with funky new bars which serve plates of starters as canapés to accompany your campari from around 1900. Many of these bars are sponsored by Martini who have invented the local concept of the 'drinner' (a Martini or two with food and music). These bars become the city's late lounges with St Germain and their imitators turned up high on the speakers.

When it comes to clubbing in Turin, don't expect the stereotype V-neck and brogues, vanity and slightly dodgy techno of Milan and other Italian cities. Some mediocre discos do exist in town but Turin's edge is its grungy youth culture based around reggae, drum'n'bass and jazz. The late hour meccas are the Po-side Murazzi, where former boathouses have been transformed into back-to-back riverside clubs (many of which are only open in summer), and the jazz venues of the Docks Dora in the northwest. Traditional discos are usually open until 0400 in the morning, as are the clubs in the Murazzi and Dora areas although some of these seem to stay open until the last person leaves. This alternative scene is the heartbeat and barometer of Turin. Many venues are linked to associations such as ARCI and AICS, associations for which in theory a yearly pass is required in order to gain entry. This is obtainable immediately on the door but may cost more than you want to pay. As a temporary visitor, if you take some ID with you and are prepared to leave it on the door, that should suffice for free entry. If they look like resisting, plead your case as a foreigner and newcomer to Turin. They'll want to show you the place and make a good impression. Entry into bars is always free; discos and nightclubs can cost anything from € 10-15 at the cheap end to € 20-25 for places like Hennessey.

Centre

Bars

Mulassano, piazza Castello 15. *Open all day until 0100. Map 2, D7, p253* Retaining the atmosphere of the bars where the first vermouths were drunk (see box, p171) this little, atmospheric café/bar is covered in mirrors, bronzes and marble furnishings. It is known for its superb *tramezzini* (sandwich snacks), invented here, and with fillings such as lobster.

★ **Bars**

Best
- Ambhara, p173
- Café Blu, p174
- Doctor Sax, p169
- Giancarlo, p170
- L'Hennessey, p169

Northeast

Bars

Antica Enoteca del Borgo, via Monferrato 4. *Open 1900-000. Map 2, D13, p253* This wine bar is a buzzy place at aperitif time and has a great selection of wines.

L'Aperitivo, C.so Alcide De Gasperi 57. *Open 1800-0100. Map 3, E3, p254* As the name suggests, a pre-dinner hotspot, famous for attracting local celebs.

Bar 21, piazza Vittorio Veneto 21. *Open 1800-0100. Map 2, D10, p253* Under La Mole, the tables of this trendy bar look like ice blocks. Absinthe is on the drinks menu.

Caffe Elena, piazza Vittorio Veneto 5. *Map 2, D11, p253 See also Eating, p146.* This is currently one of the most in vogue hang-outs at aperitif time.

La Drogheria, piazza Vittorio Veneto 18. *Open 1900-2300. Map 2, D11, p253* Super-crowded at aperitif time by students and ex-pats, this is currently one of the hippest bars with a great view over piazza Vittorio and the hillside across the Po. Among the canapés is *mini-bagna cauda*.

Clubs

Arcate 10 e 12, Murazzi del Po 10-12. *Open summer only, 1900-0200. Map 2, C12, p253* A spacious and lively bar in prime riverside location spanning two sets of former boathouse arches.

The Beach, Murazzi del Po, 18-20-22. *Open 2000-0300. Map 2, C12, p253* Ambitiously named but a nice mellow chill-out bar with plenty of tables by the riverside in summer.

Bockaos, Murazzi del Po 2. *Open 2000-0300. Map 2, D12, p253* Newly installed next to its more illustrious neighbour *Doctor Sax*, worth popping in on during the Murazzi club crawl.

Doctor Sax, Murazzi del Po 4. *Open 2000-0400. Map 2, D12, p253* The longest standing and still the best of the former boathouse clubs in the Murazzi, a perennial favourite with Turin's immigrant population and therefore serious about its reggae and African vibes. Great decor with the chassis and seats of an old tram lining the interconnecting corridor. Live music during the week and occasional stripteases.

L'Hennessey, strada Traforo del Pino 23, **T**011 8998522. *Open 2200-0400. Map 1, A8, p250* Of Turin's traditional disco-type nightclubs, this is the best with a smooth clientele of beautiful people grooving to the latest tunes that are more Ibiza than Italian old skool.

Pier 7-9-11, Murazzi del Po. *Open 2000-0300. Map 2, C12, p253* One of the clubs in the Murazzi with a more elegant decor and clientele. Frenetic dancing outside when the weather's right.

Southeast

Bars

The Shamrock Inn, C.so Vittorio Emanuele II, 34, **T** 011 8174950.
Open 1930-0100. Map 2, H8, p253 If you must go to an Irish pub in
Turin, then go to this one. They're actually more popular among
Italians than ex-pats. The advantage with Italian licensing laws is
that they can stay open much later than British versions. The
Shamrock is pretty authentic, not just with the Guinness, but with
a fun, packed and brawly atmosphere.

Clubs

Alcatraz, Murazzi del Po 37/41, **T** 0349 8053516. *Open 2130-0300.
Map 2, F12, p253* The bare walls and dungeon feel surely evoke the
infamous prison in this, one of Turin's most popular bar/clubs.

Aqua, Murazzi del Po 31/33. *Open 2000-0200. Map 2, E12, p253*
Water by name and location, a good club but essentially
indistinguishable from the nearby riverside haunts.

Arcata 35, Murazzi del Po 35. *Open summer only, 1900-0100. Map
2, E12, p253* Literally 'arch number 35' in this long chain of
bar/clubs sharing the same atmospheric architecture.

Café Tabac, Murazzi del Po 3, **T** 011 8123381. *Open
1900-0100. Map 2, D12, p253* A murky and atmospheric bar/
restaurant with vaulted bare-brick arched interior. Also good for
brunch at weekends.

Giancarlo, Murazzi del Po 43. *Open 2000-0400. Map 2, F12, p253*
Second to *Doctor Sax*, this is one of the more long-standing of the

▶ Martini shaken or stirred?

The word vermouth derives from the German, Wermut, for absinthe, the alcohol that had first been invented by Hippocrates in Ancient Greece and which had been enhanced in the Middle Ages by spices from the Far East and Americas. It was vintner Antonio Benedetto Carpano in Turin who in the 18th century decided to add herbal aromas to the alcoholic base using recipes provided for him by the local monks. The new drink went down a storm and in 1773 Vittorio Amedeo II made it the court drink. Carpano founded a company on the back of his success, called *Punt e Mes*, and other people soon jumped on the bandwagon with their own versions of the brew, notably a Mr Cinzano and a Mr Martini, so that now the generic drink vermouth accounts for a quarter of all Italy's wine exports. The base is 75% white wine added to a neutral liquid that is aromatized with a combination of herbs, each company having its different combination. Whether it is white or red depends on the addition of colouring. You will see a type of vermouth being very commonly drunk in Turin, especially at aperitif time, at the bar stacked high with olives, cold meats and cheeses. But perhaps vermouth's most important role has been in providing the base for a number of famous cocktails, notably the *Negroni*, with Campari and gin, the *Manhattan* with angostura bitters and whisky, the *Bacardi Symphony*, combined with rum and Grand Marnier and most famously, mixed with vodka, shaken or stirred.

Murazzi venues, spread out over many floors and high-ceilinged brick-vaulted halls, always heaving with underground youth. Music varies from reggae to Italian rock and drum'n'bass.

Jammin', Murazzi del Po 1/19. *Open 1930-0230.* *Map 2, D12, p253*
Afro-inspired club playing predominantly reggae and other
Caribbean/African music.

Olé Madrid, Murazzi del Po 5. *Open 1900-0200.* *Map 2, D12, p253*
A lively bar-cum-nightclub under the arches with a Spanish flavour
in both the snack menu and music. Also serves good pizzas.

Pot-Able, Murazzi del Po 53. *Open 2000-0200.* *Map 2, F12, p253*
A lively watering hole and a relaxed, refreshing change from the
heaving throng in the other clubs along the Murazzi.

Puddhu bar, Murazzi del Po 21. *Open 1900-0300.* *Map 2, E12, p253*
Turin's answer to the Paris *Buddha Bar*, with a zen-inspired decor
and playing mellow music to drink and sink back to.

Southwest

Bars

Norman, via Pietro Micca 22. *Map 2, D5, p252* A luxurious bar
which attracts the pre- and post-show crowd from the Alfieri
theatre. Thursday-Saturday it is open all night.

Notorius, via Stradella 10/d. *Map 1, C3, p250* One of Turin's most
popular dance venues with a speciality in themed revival nights.

Clubs

Sabor Latino, via Stradella 10, **T** 011 852327. *Open 2000-0200. Map
2, A4, p252* A steamy Latin bar mixing Caribbean grooves, salsa
and other jives spurred on by sensuous in-house dancers.

Supermarket, via Madonna di Campagna 1. *Open 2200-0400. Map 1, C2, p250* A dancefloor that also becomes an expo space for new and avant-garde live music in a converted cinema.

Heaven. *Open 2200-0400. Map 4, p256* Out towards Stupinigi, this is Italian clubbing at its most stereotypical (and awful). Techno compilations being sung to in unison by group of tactile sweaty teenage males with inappropriately beautiful girlfriends.

Da Giau, strada Castello di Mirafiori 346, **T** 011 6060753. *Open 2100-0500. Map 1, L5, p251* One of Turin's grungiest and hippiest venues, an oddball combination of gothic and thrash dancefloor, board and card games and plenty of drinking in a venue that is at turns oddly brightly lit and murky, and always full of characters.

Northwest

Bars

L'Albero di Vino, piazza della Consolata 9. *Open 1900-0100. Map 2, B4, p252* A popular wine bar on this atmospheric and revitalized little square serving an excellent selection of wines for all tastes and times of the day.

Ambhara Bar, via Borgo Dora 10, **T** 011 5217346. *Open 1900-0200. Map 2, A4, p252* One of Turin's newest and trendiest at the time of going to press. Fusion cuisine and a good mix of cocktails, aperitifs and regional wines.

Arancia di Mezzanotte, piazza E. Filibert 11. *Open 1800-0100. Map 2, B4, p252* Less an array of aperitif canapés than a whole buffet, you will be doing well to have an appetite after a few drinks here. Trendy young clientele and open late.

Bacaro, piazza della Consolata 1. *Open 1900-0100.* *Map 2, B4, p252* A popular aperitif bar in the heart of the *quadrilatero romano*.

Barbaru, via San Dalmazzo 8/a. *Open 1900-0100.* *Map 2, C4, p252* Clean and contemporary wine bar in the New York mould.

Barolino Cocchi, via Bonelli 16/c. *Open 1900-0100.* *Map 2, B4, p252* A bar for architecture enthusiasts who can enjoy an aperitif or a late-night chaser in an historic oval-shaped space designed by Filippo Juvarra.

Birrificio di Torino, via Parma 30, **T** 011 2876562. *Open 1900-2300.* *Map 2, A8, p253* A bright and lively bar serving a wide variety of international beers.

Brasserie Societe Lutece, piazza Carlo Emanuele II 21. *Open 1930-2300.* *Map 2, D9, p253* Another popular haunt at aperitif time with a jovial informal atmosphere. You can also eat here.

Café Blu, via Valprato 68, **T** 011 280251. *Open 2100-0230.* *Map 1, C4, p250* Music for all tastes on different nights in one of Turin's most fashionable 'underground' clubs. Hard rock, house and ska.

Docks Arte, via Valprato 68. *Open until 0400.* *Map 1, C4, p250* One of the many unusual venues in these converted warehouses with jazz, exhibitions and DJ nights in constant evolution.

Docks Home, via Valprato 68, **T** 0347 4210989. *Open until 0400.* *Map 1, C4, p250* A temple for the latest mixes of house and techno, but which also lays on enormous plates of aperitif snacks on Tuesdays. Thursdays are more rock'n'roll. Tessera AICS membership needed, although you may be able to bypass this as a temporary visitor.

Dual, cia Cesare Battisti 17/d. *Open 2030-0200.* *Map 2, D7, p253*
Very influenced by New York, this is a bar for trendy and affluent
thirtysomethings with revival house music most nights, and
occasional piano bar. Busy at aperitif time.

Fish, via Valerio 5/b. *Open 1900-0100.* *Map 2, A4, p252* A popular
aperitif bar with a surrealist-inspired themed decor.

Hiroshima mon amour, via Bossoli 83, **T** 011 317427. *Open
2100-0400.* *Map 1, I7, p251* A reference point in Turin's
nightscape for decades, a grungy mecca for rock, reggae and
techno nights.

Luce e Gas, via IV Marzo 21/c. *Open 1930-0200.* *Map 2, C5, p252*
Aperitif, dinner and after-dark all rolled into one, with lounge tunes
on the ground floor and a post-ecclesiastical retro vibe in the
converted crypt restaurant in the basement.

Il lupo della steppa, via San Domenico. *Map 2, C3, p252* Hermann
Hesse has long been revered by Italian hippies and this bohemian
joint, evoking his novel *Steppenwolf*, is a mellow venue for jazz,
cocktails and Viennese cakes.

I Magazzini Reddocks, via Valprato 68, open until 0500, AICS
tessera, free on Fridays. *Map 1, C4, p250* An unusual multi-arts
venue in a converted warehouse with concerts, film projections
and dancing featuring local DJs.

Mood, via Cesare Battisti. *Open 1930-2300.* *Map 2, D7, p253* Good
for aperitifs with the locals.

Paris Texas, piazza IV Marco. *Open 1900-0100.* *Map 2, C5, p252*
Seventies-influenced retro bar big on loud colours and plastics.

Pastis, piazza E. Filiberto 9/b. *Open 1900-0100.* *Map 2, B4, p252* A stylish place to kick-start the evening with a Ricard or other aperitifs.

Las Rosas, via Bellezia 15/f, **T** 011 5213907. *Open 1930-2300.* *Map 2, C4, p252* Mexican-flavoured tapas and cocktails.

La Rusnenta, via Vittorio Andreis 11, **T** 011 4362980. *Open 1930-2300.* *Map 2, A4, p252* A traditional Piemontese restaurant where the work of local artists provides a constantly changing and innovative decor.

Turin has a fine tradition of arts and is also an unsuspected hub of stimulating contemporary arts. The permanent exhibition space at Torino Esposizioni in the parco Valentino is a constant reference point for a wide variety of exciting cultural trade fairs and exhibitions. Arts information is readily available on the walls and in the cafés around the university district north of via Po, from the tourist office on piazza Castello, daily in the back pages of the Turin newspaper, *La Stampa* or best of all in its weekly cultural supplement, *Torino Sette*, which comes out every Friday and provides complete listings and features. There is also a good Italian website, www.torinospettacoli.it, for the latest news on shows, timings of performances, ticket bookings and prices. There is also a good guide called *News Spettacolo Torino*, available free from street stands, which, in addition to arts news, has information on clubs, bars and pop concerts.

Cinema

As befits the home of Italian cinema, the city is well stocked with cinemas and in October hosts the annual **Festival di Cinema Giovane** in various arthouse cinemas around town, aimed at finding the new Fellini. The voices of film dubbers are as famous as many actors in Italy as most films are dubbed, occasionally subtitled and rarely in the original language on selected evenings.

The following are all multi-screen cinemas where the latest Italian and international blockbusters are on show, while the newspapers mentioned above have details of screenings of art-house films in the city's small cinemas:

Greenwich Village, via Po 30, **T** 011 8173323. *Map 2, D9, p253* **Medusa Multicinema**, C.so Umbria 60, **T** 011 1975757. *Map 1, D3, p250* **Ambrosio**, C.so Vittorio Emanuele 52, **T** 011 547007. *Map 2, H5, p252* **Ideal**, C.so Beccaria 4, **T** 011 52143116. *Map 2, C1, p252* **Pathe Multiplex**, C.so Montevecchio 39, **T** 011 5189858. *Map 3, B3, p254*

Contemporary art

Away from the regular museums, Turin has countless impromptu and temporary venues for art exhibitions, either in the loft spaces of post-industrial regeneration areas or in the city's many former *case nobili* which private owners or the local council make available. The local council is particularly energetic in sponsoring arts events aimed at raising the city's cultural profile, most recently with the annual city-wide installation art movement *Luci d'Artista*. The following are a number of addresses and institutions particularly worth visiting:

Carbone.to, via dei Mille 38, **T** 011 8395911. *Map 2, F9, p253* A showcase for current trends in Italian contemporary art.

Fondazione Sandretto Re Rebaudengo, via Modane 16, www.fondsrr.org **T** 011 19831600. *Map 3, F1, p254* A multi-faceted space aimed at showing the best of what's making waves on the continent. It also has a bookshop, restaurant and internet café.

In Arco, piazza Vittorio Veneto 1, **T** 011 882208. *Map 2, D11, p253* Fine temporary exhibitions of post-war international art.

Photo & Contemporary, via dei Mille 36, **T** 011 889884. *Map 2, G9, p253* The best of the latest world photography.

Popular music

In terms of more modern artistic idioms, Turin is acknowledged as the Italian capital of jazz and also of a burgeoning local style of roots reggae, while the city is a guaranteed multi-date destination on the tours of famous Italian and international bands. Turin- formed bands making waves in Italy and in other corners of continental Europe are Mau Mau, Subsonica and Africa Unite. See Bars and clubs, p165, for details of live music venues.

Theatre, opera and classical music

Operas such as *Tosca* were premiered in Turin and the Teatro Regio, part of the regal architecture of piazza Castello, is a famous destination on the international concert, opera and ballet calendar. The main theatres belong to an association called *Teatro Stabile Torino*. Information and listings information on these theatres is available from www.teatrostabiletorino.it The provincial theatre of the Piemontese dialect is alive in Turin and the city has many outlets specifically aimed at nurturing new local and Italian talent.

Alfa Teatro, via Casalborgone 16/1, **T** 011 8193529. *Map 1, C8, p250* A beautiful little theatre with a 1928 Viennese interior which hosts music, jazz, readings, operettas and dance shows.

Auditorium Giovanni Agnelli, via Nizza 280, Lingotto **T** 011 6640458. *Map 1, J6, p251* Part of the Agnelli artistic patrimony in the Lingotto ex-Fiat complex and a venue for classical music, particularly chamber music.

Conservatorio Giuseppe Verdi, piazza Bodoni 63, **T** 011 8178458. *Map 2, G8, p253* Aside from the Teatro Regio, this is the main reference point for concerts and music recitals.

Gioello Teatro, via Colombo 31/b, **T** 011 6615447. *Map 3, D4, p254* Located in an old cinema, this little theatre concentrates on the works of new Italian playwrights.

Teatro Alfieri, piazza Solferino 2, **T** 011 5623800. *Map 2, E4, p252* A classic on the Turin theatre landscape, hosting plays by Wilde and Brecht as well as unusual 20th drama from the likes of Boris Vian.

Teatro Araldo/Teatro dell'Angolo, via Chiomonte 3, **T** 011 4899676. *Map 1, G3, p251* Turin's main theatre showing plays for and including children.

Teatro Carignano, via Maria Vittoria 5, **T** 011 541136. *Map 2, E7, p253* Good for music recitals, classical plays and religious music.

Teatro Colosseo, via Madama Cristina 71, **T** 011 6698034. *Map 3, C9, p255* A reference point for cabarets, musicals and music recitals.

Teatro Erba, C.so Moncalieri 241, **T** 011 6615447. *Map 3, B12, p255* Allied to the Gioiello and Alfieri theatres and showing similar plays and spectacles.

Teatro Gianduja, via Santa teresa 5, **T** 011 530238.   *Map 2, E6, p252*   The place to go for puppet shows and also if you want to watch theatre in dialect.

Teatro Gobetti, via Rossini 8, **T** 011 5169412.   *Map 2, C9, p253*   The traditional home of Shakespeare plays in Turin.

Teatro Juvarra, via Juvarra 15, **T** 011 540675.   *Map 2, D2, p252*   Specializing in experimental and avant-garde theatre and performance art.

Teatro Matteotti, via Matteotti 1, Moncalieri, **T** 011 6403700. *Map 1, K8, p251*   A provincial arm of the Carignano specializing in 20th theatre from around the world.

Teatro Nuovo, C.so Massimo d'Azeglio, **T** 011 6500200.   *Map 3, E10, p255*   Famous for its dance and operetta shows, with a revered dance and theatre school attached.

Teatro Regio, piazza Castello 215, **T** 011 8815241, www.teatroregio.it *Map 2, C7, p253*   Turin's most prestigious theatre, opera and concert hall.

Festivals and events

Turin is not Italy's most exuberant city when it comes to festivals – it lives up to its stereotype as a rather restrained, serious and hard-working city where, so people say, the prevalence of gloaming weather extinguishes the sun-dependent Mediterranean spirit. Even the almost annual triumph of Juventus in the Serie A football championship seems to pass uncelebrated, as if entirely predictable. Like most Mediterranean countries, Italy has its fair share of Saint's days and Feast Days but in Turin these, alongside the National Liberation Day and Unification Day, represent a day off work rather than a cause for more elaborate celebration. Piedmont redresses the balance out in the provinces, where the rural sense of tradition, folklore and nature's priorities come to the fore in some of Italy's most riotous and tasty parties. Precise dates for the following festivals and events change year on year, so contact the relevant tourist office for precise information.

February

Carnevale d'Ivrea (late Feb/early Mar) Valencia and Nice may have their tomato-throwing festivals, but oranges go faster and further and do more damage, which is what makes Ivrea's three days of citrus anarchy in the lead up to Mardi Gras one of the best weekends available in Italy. It's all based on medieval folklore but then it had to be, and if it wasn't then you'd have to invent it. See also page 115.

March

CioccolaTò (6-23) Using a play on words with *cioccolato* and *Tò* denoting Turin, this new festival is entirely dedicated to the god of cocoa. Almost a whole month of events takes place involving good food, wine, music, literature, cinema and art throughout the Piedmont region, all inspired by chocolate. Turin is in fact one of the noble homelands of this delicacy, imported into Italy centuries ago by Emanuele Filiberto of Savoy. See also www.cioccola-to.it

April

Turin Gay and Lesbian Film Festival. Every year in April the city hosts this film festival. April 2004 will be the 19th edition. For more information visit www.tglff.com

Turin Marathon One of Italy's more famous and scenic marathons, taking place in April each year. For further information, contact via Ventimiglia 145, **T** 011 6631231, www.turinmarathon.it

May

Fiera del Libro (early May) One of the main events on Turin's cultural calendar, the annual four-day book fair is held in the

Torino Esposizioni exhibition hall. Publishers from all over Italy, including Turin-based Einaudi, come to display their latest books. The fair has an trade-oriented edge but is meant to be primarily for the public, with events and kids activities. www.fieralibro.it/eng

September

Il Palio di Asti In September revellers descend on the city of Asti for the local version of the Palio horse race that has made Siena so famous. While the event takes place in a piazza that is for the rest of the year a large car park, it still has all the passion, folklore and risk of its Tuscan cousin.

Settembre Musica The most famous, complete and sumptuous festival of classical music. This festival brings the very best international musicians to the capital of Piedmont and recently added a few concerts of avant-garde, contemporary, jazz and ethnic music. www.settembremusica.it/english/index.htm

Jazz festival Watch out for outdoor live events throughout the month in parks as well as live jazz in the city's many bars.

October

Torino Film Festival (mid Nov) This is the second most important Italian cinema festival after Venice and has become a reference point for emerging directors from all over the world. The site for the festival has recently changed to the modern multiplex Pathé at the Lingotto centre. The event gets richer by the year. For further information see www.torinofilmfest.org

Il Palio dell'Asino di Alba For centuries Alba and Asti have been neighbours and rivals. This is no better expressed than in the irony with which Alba conducts its parody of Asti's *Palio*. Merciless

When in the Roman quarter…

Act like the torinese and head for the characterful streetside bars and cafés.

amusement is caused by the sight of awkward donkeys entering into what could only be charitably called a race around the main square.

Festa delle Trofie In October gourmets from all over the world descend on Alba to celebrate, sniff out and buy the white gold of Italian cuisine, the white truffle, just that much more powerful, rich and rare than its black cousin. Market stalls celebrate and sell the truffles while the local restaurant rake it in with all manner of delicious but highly prized and priced dishes containing miserly shavings of the stuff.

Salone del Gusto (21-25 in 2004) The 'taste fair' is one of the biggest and most important food and wine events in the world, organised by the Slow Food Association every two years at the Lingotto. Producers display and sell goods and visitors can participate in tasting, debates and even meet some famous international personages. See also www.slowfood.com

---

November

Luci d'Artista (early Nov-mid Jan) An open-air exhibition that is becoming well-known at an international level, promoting Turin as the capital of contemporary art. Installations are by both Italian and foreign artists, including recently Rebecca Horn, Joseph Kosuth, Daniel Buren and Jan Vercruysse.

Artissima (early Nov) The international fair of contemporary art occupies a unique position among European art fairs. This four-day fair is exclusively dedicated to contemporary art and the newest art trends, with an established international character and a very high standard. For more information see www.artissima.it

Like most Italian cities, Turin is a shopper's paradise and all the major labels are represented down the catwalk streets of via Roma and via Lagrange. But with the stigma of Fiat and heavy industry, not many would know that Turin was once Italy's fashion capital, a mantle that has since passed on to Florence and now Milan. Turin is also a paradise for gastronomes, especially those with a sweet tooth, and also for antique-hunters, where along via Maria Vittoria and around via Borgo Dora, you'll find some unusual bric-à-brac.

With the advent of the Euro, prices are not as low as they used to be relative to Great Britain, but leather goods in particular are still good value. Also, especially in smaller and more expensive shops, it is impossible to browse without being accosted by an inquiring, and slightly snooty, shop assistant.

Shops are normally open from 0830 in the morning with all but the large department stores closing for an hour, sometimes more, for lunch between 1230-1430, staying open until 1900.

Antiques

Bolaffi, via Cavour 17. *Map 2, F8, p253* Stamps and rare posters.

Delfa Loqui, via Maria Vittoria 22/c. *Map 2, E8, p253* For Meissen china.

Fiore Antichita, via Maria Vittoria 36/c. *Map 2, E7, p253* Sculptures, paintings and furniture from the 18th and 19th centuries.

Gioelleria Mangia, via Amendola 14. *Map 2, E7, p253* Silverware and jewellery, specializing in French and English styles and services.

Libreria Antiquaria Freddi, via San Massimo 34/h. *Map 2, G9, p253* First editions of Italian, French and avant-garde works.

Libreria Antiquaria Little Nemo, via Montebello 2. *Map 2, C9, p253* Rare illustrated books including many cartoon volumes.

Yesterday, via Petrarca 11/c. *Map 3, E9, p255* Furniture and silverware from the 18th and 19th centuries.

Books

Arethusa, via Po 2. *Map 2, C8, p253* The place to go to read up on 'Black Magic Turin'.

Drueto, piazza CLN 223. *Map 2, F6, p252* Specialist stockist of art and architecture books since 1925.

Figuriamoci, via San Massimo 2/b. *Map 2, F10, p253* Specializing in cartoon books.

Jules et Jim, via Bogino 19. *Map 2, D8, p253* Named after the famous Truffaut film, an excellent store for cinema-related books and also old and new film magazines and posters.

Luxembourg, via Principe Amedeo 29. *Map 2, D8, p253* A good place for English, American and other foreign fiction.

Mondadori Multicenter, via Viotti. *Map 2, D6, p252* 1500 sq m of books, CDs and DVDs.

Mood, **Libri & Caffe**, via Cesare Batisti 3/e. *Map 2, D7, p253* Café and book shop. Very intellectual. Very cool.

Nucleon, via Bellezia 15/b. *Map 2,C4, p252* Art book shop and expo space.

Oolp, via Principe Amedeo 29. *Map 2,D8,p253* Charing Cross Road transported to Turin, especially for new, second-hand and rare books.

Paravia, via Garibaldi 23. *Map 2, D3, p253* Well-known book shop for almost everything.

Feltrinelli, piazza Castello 17, **T** 011 541627. *Map 2, C7, p253* Recently refurbished and excellent.

Clothes

Brooksfield, via Gobetti 10. *Map 2, F7, p253* Classic English style clothes made in Moncalieri over three floors.

EtaBeta, via Principi d'Acaja 51, **T** 011 4340008. *Map 1, F4, p250* Most designer labels at knock-down prices.

Kristina Ti, via Mari Vittoria 18/9.   *Map 2, E8, p253* Made in Turin, specializing in slinky swimwear.

Mondo, via Roma 247.   *Map 2, E7, p253* All the major designer labels for man and woman, plus a range of perfumes and household decorations.

Rao, via Andrea Doria 8.   *Map 2, F8, p253* Traditional formal wear for men. The women's store is in via Lagrange 6.

Scooter, piazza Paleocapa 2.   *Map 2, G6, p252* Grunge and stylish youth clothes from France.

Top Ten, via Soleri 2.   *Map 2, F7, p253* Unusual designer labels and expensive clothes for man and woman.

Vertice, via Lagrange 15.   *Map 2, E7, p253* Dior, Dolce, Versace and friends.

Department stores

Rinascente, via Lagrange 15.   *Map 2, E7, p253* Favourite place for trysts between Turin's amorous adolescents.

San Carlo dal 1973, via Roma 53.   *Map 2, D6, p252* All-in-one. Clothes, crafts, food and chic household goods. Turin's first concept store.

Design

Full Full, via Castelnuovo 14.   *Map 1, D7, p250* Designs from young designers that don't make it to mass production.

Galleria One Off, via Bonelli 3. *Map 2, B4, p252* A shop-cum-expo space for young Turin designers.

Food

Abrate, via Po 10. *Map 2, D8, p253* Recently reopened with a restored interior laden with tooth decaying delicacies.

Baita del Formagg, via Lagrange 36. *Map 2, F7, p253* A cheese paradise from all over the world.

Baudracco, C.so Vittorio Emanuele II. *Map 2, H6, p252* Meats from small local producers.

Bersano, via Barbaroux 5. *Map 2, C5, p252* All manner of breads and enormous *grissini*.

Borgiattino Formaggi, via Cernaia 32. *Map 2, E4, p252* Specializing in delectable Piemontese cheese.

Casa del Barolo, via Andrea Doria 7. *Map 2, G8, p253* The ultimate for local wines, including the famous Barolo.

Cremeria Ghigo, via Po 52. *Map 2, G9, p253* The unmissable address for the famous local chocolates and sweets.

El Formage, via Garibaldi 41. *Map 2, D9, p253* Pâtés and cheeses practically designed to ensure cholesterol and therefore very nice.

Ficini, via Berthollet 30. *Map 3, A8, p255* Bread, nuts, olives and excellent grissini.

Fiorio, via Po 8. *Map 2, D8, p253* One of the city's most famous places for ice cream.

Miretti, C.so Matteotti 5. *Map 2, G5, p252* Great for ice cream but also *zabaglione* and *fior di panna*.

La Montagna in Vetrina, piazza Emanuele Filiberto 3. *Map 2, B4, p252* Claims to be an agriturismo in the city, and more than lives up to it. Wonderful variety of sumptuous rural flavours.

Parola, C.so Vittorio Emanuele II 76. *Map 2, H8, p253* A 100 years of wineselling also with great grappas and ratafia.

Pasticceria Gerla, C.so Vittorio Emanuele II 88. *Map 2, H4, p252* Up and running since 1927, this shop boasts 42 types of homemade chocolates.

Pasticceria Gertosio, via Lagrange 24/h. *Map 2, G7, p253* Hansel and Gretel, life is a box of chocolates, child in a sweetshop...

Pepino, piazza Carignano 8. *Map 2, D7, p253* Famous for its 'penguin' ice cream, a Turin regular since 1937.

Premier Cioccolato-Caleagno, via Bersezio5. *Map 1, C5, p250* Mouthwatering assortment of gianduiotti, pralines, noisettes and chocolate creams.

Rosada, via Magenta 10. *Map 2, H6, p252* Selling a delicious selection of meats.

Salumeria Bettin Chabert, via Po 18. *Map 2, D/C9, p253* All manner of heavenly cheeses, meat and fish under the arcades.

Stratta, piazza San Carlo 191. *Map 2, E7, p253* Mouthwatering *gianduja* and other bonbons.

Shopping

Glassware

Jose Ferrer, via XX Settembre. *Map 2, E6, p252* Specializes in Daum crystal.

Herbal and flowers

Grand Madre Natura, via Santore di Santarosa 7/b. *Map 1, E7, p250* The green shop in Turin stocking bio-everything.

La Vie en Rose, via Accademia Albertina 35. *Map 2, E9, p253* Spectacular roses.

Tulip Company, piazza Vittorio Veneto 9. *Map 2, D11, p253* Selling flowers from Holland and also interesting plant-based furniture and decorations.

Jewellery

Pisano, via Bogino 10/f. *Map 2, D8, p253* Come here if you happen to need an expensive, unusual watch or want to buy a special present for a loved one.

Leisurewear and designer label warehouse stores

Basic Village, via Foggia 42. *Map 1, C5, p250* Specializing in Kappa clothes.

Carrera Jeans, via XX Settembre 71, Collegno, **T** 011 4037727. *Map 2, A6, p252* What it says on the tin.

Diffusione Tessile, C.so Francia 313, **T** 011 4157840. *Map 1, E3, p250* Knock-down labels for ladies.

Il Grifoncino, via Bodoni 5, **T** 011 8179260. *Map 2, G8, p253* Ralph Lauren et al at sensible prices.

Il Guardaroba, via Massena 7, **T** 011 501122. *Map 2, G6, p252* Valentino and Versace at a discount.

Invicta, C.so Toscana 13/15, Venaria Reale, **T** 011 730231. *Map 1, C1, p250* For those love 'em or hate 'em school rucksacks.

Superga, via Reimondo 23/b, Rivoli, **T** 011 9565511. For the plimsoles and pumps de rigueur in summer for Italian teenagers.

Lingerie

Gimo, via Goilitti. *Map 2, E8, p253* Designer underwear laid out on antique furniture which is also for sale.

Music

Augusta, via Po 3. *Map 2, C8, p253* The store for classical music fans.

Maschio, piazza Castello 43. *Map 2, C7, p253* CDs and DVDs of virtually everything.

Ricordi Mediastore, via Roma 255. *Map 2, D7, p253* The Turin branch of the Virgin-style music temple.

Perfumes

Artisan Parfumeur, via Mazzini 26. *Map 2, G8, p253* A famous perfumier stocking recherché scents from the 19th century.

Galleria San Federico, galleria San Federico 28.   *Map 2, G8,
p253*   English perfumes from the 19th and early 20th century such
as Floris and Penhaligons.

Shoes and bags

Bertolini & Borse, piazza Vittorio Veneto 8.   *Map 2, D11,
p253*   Open since 1923, this classy shop sells bags, accessories and
other leather goods.

Bruschi, piazza San Carlo 208.   *Map 2, E6, p252*   Prada, Valentino
and Versace at a classy address.

Cavagna, via Accademia delle Scienze.   *Map 2, D7, p253*   Gloves of
all finishes and sizes since 1954.

Regina, via Villa della Regina.   *Map 1, E7, p250*   Designer shoes.

Shoeco, piazza Carlo Emanuele II 19.   *Map 2, E9, p253*
Off-the-wall shoe designs.

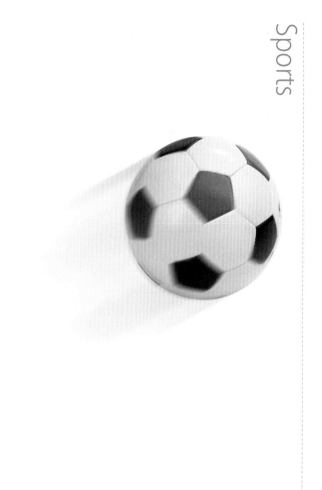

As befits an Olympic city that is also home to Juventus and Torino football clubs, Turin is sport mad. The scarves, flags, strips and graffiti of the famous black and white and *granata* (purple) teams are visible and on sale at every corner kiosk. Juventus are yet again champions of Italy and hold the record for the most championships titles. Their Stadio delle Alpi is rarely full for normal games but tickets for games against the rival Milan teams, Italian Cup games, the twice-yearly derby and European games are by contrast usually very hard to get hold of. The parco Valentino and the parco Pellerina are full of impromptu games, with players trying to bend it like Del Piero, and it is very easy to join in. Football is not the only sport however. Turin has plenty of gyms and pools as well as facilities for those other Italian sporting obsessions: cycling, basketball and volleyball. The rolling plains and hills of Piedmont provide great trails for hiking and mountain biking, as well as many golf courses. Turin is also Italy's skiing capital, with ten or more world-famous resorts on its doorstep.

2006 Winter Olympics

For all information regarding the forthcoming Olympics contact Committee for the **Organisation of Winter Olympics**, via Nizza 262/58, **T** 011 6310511, www.torino2006.org See also box, p85.

Bungee jumping

If you fancy falling from a great height voluntarily, try the bungee jumping centre at Veglio-Mosso 90 km away between Turin and Milan, **T** 848 580114 or **T** 015 702488, www.bungee.it At € 78 a leap, the view is of a lush wooded valley from a high river bridge.

Cycling

Turin has over 40 km of cycle tracks. Particularly scenic are those alongside the Po and Dora riverbanks. The main parks of Pellerina, Mandria and Valentino also provide for nice rambles and bicycles are available for hire. For bike hire, see Directory, p216.

Equestrianism

To ride horses or watch horse racing go to the complex at via Stupinigi 182, **T** 011 9651356/57/58.

Football

Turin's **Stadio delle Alpi**, strada Comunlale di Altessano, is the local temple to football, located about 30 minutes from the city centre. League games are played on Sundays with Juventus currently on top of Serie A and Torino languishing below in Serie B. See also box, p97.

Tickets for Serie A games at the Stadio delle Alpi can be obtained by ringing the stadium itself, by contacting the club HQs themselves and also at some of the major newspaper kiosks in town, such as on the corner of via Nizza. Alternatively, tickets can be obtained by contacting **Juventus Club**, C.so Galileo Ferraris 32, **T** 011 65631, www.juventus.com, *Map 2, H4, p252*; **Torino Calcio**, via del Carmin 29, **T** 011 5712211, www.toro.it, *Map 2, C2, p252*; or the **Toro Biglietteria**, via Alioni 3, **T** 011 5217049, *Map 2, B1, p252.*

The best way to actually play some football is to join in one of the spontaneous and quite competitive games that are often being played among friends and strangers in the city's main parks.

Golf

One- or three day golf passes (€ 25 or € 60 accordingly, buy from tourist information) are available for use on most of the courses in and around Turin. The price includes the use of a bag and clubs. You will probably need to demonstrate your official handicap when buying a pass. The following are a few of the city's golf clubs:

Golf Club I Girasoli, via Pralormo 315, Carmagnola, **T** 011 9795088. Open course, par 65 at 5,000 m.

Golf Club la Margherita, via Pralormo, Carmagnola, **T** 011 9795113. By far the longest course. Agriturismo accommodation also available.

Circolo Golf Torino, via Grange 137, Fiano Torinese, **T** 011 9235440. Green, flat, open course.

Moncalieri Golf Club, strada Vallere 20, Moncalieri, **T** 011 641695. Green, flat, open course.

Gyms

Playtime, via Lagrange 27-29, **T** 011 5620520, *Map 2, G7, p253*.
With weights galore plus specialist classes for all the fitness fads
from yoga to pilates. They also offer a free trial week. For details on
gyms contact www.anidride.it/torino/life/palestre

Running

Turin's parks are *jogger centrale* in the morning, evenings and
weekends. Turin also hosts one of Italy's more famous and scenic
marathons, taking place in April each year. The organization
behind this is based at via Ventimiglia 145, **T** 011 6631231,
www.turinmarathon.it

Skiing

The famous resorts within 90 minutes drive of Turin are **Cervinia**
and **Courmayeur** in the Val d'Aosta and **Sestriere** and **Sauze
d'Oulx** in the Val di Susa. All are crowded and over-developed and
none will test the advanced skier, with the exception of the slopes
of Zermatt on the Swiss side of the Matterhorn at Cervinia (take
your passport) and the upper reaches of Courmayeur heading into
Chamonix and parts of adjacent la Thuile.

If you are inclined to be frustrated both by the noisy, rather
peacock-like Italian mentality on the slopes, then head for Chamonix
proper, through the Mont Blanc tunnel, or go to the little-known
resort of Pila near Cervinia, which, although not very testing,
provides lovely long pistes through the trees. With predominantly
south-facing slopes and sheltered from the weather systems coming
from the west, Italian resorts are guaranteed suntraps but snow is
often patchy and quickly turns to slush; powder is very rare indeed.
Ski passes here used to be some of the cheaper in the Alps but with
the Euro things have become more expensive. Expect to pay around

€ 40-50 in Cervinia and Sestriere, while Pila remains a more economic option, thus adding to its charm.

Swimming

Turin is has plenty of public swimming pools, including **Centro Nuoto Torino**, C.so Sebastopoli 260, **T** 011 322448, Covered pool; **Colletta**, via Ragazzoni 5, **T** 011 284626, Open-air and covered pool; **Lido di Torino**, via Villa Glori 21, **T** 011 6615210, Open-air pool; **Pellerina**, C.so Appio Claudio 110, **T** 011 744036, Open-air pool.

Volleyball and basketball

Turin is also big on volleyball and basketball, although it is generally played in clubs requiring you to pay an annual membership.

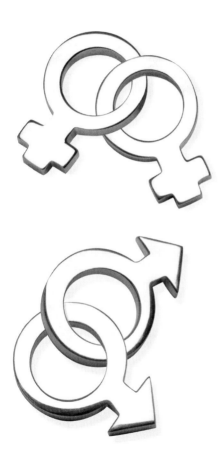

Due to its Catholic culture and the constant call of the Vatican, Italy has not traditionally been a very gay-friendly place. However, certain cities such as Bologna and Rome, ironically on the Pope's doorstep, have established significant gay communities and an accepted and explicit degree of openness. Turin is not yet at that stage although the gay community thrives in the city's significant seam of music-based underground culture and, as in many places, the gay community contributes more than its fair share towards the buzz and nightlife of the city. In this context there are a number of acknowledged meeting points and social hangouts in Turin for gay and lesbian groups and a number of websites and nationwide associations that are worth contacting for further local information.

Associations and information

The following websites are good for the latest news, events and for meeting people and more in-depth local information: www.gay.it, www.informagay.it, www.clubclassic.net/guida/torino

Circolo Maurice, via della Basilica 3/5, **T** 011 5211116 www.mauriceglbt.org *1000-1700*. *Map 2, B5, p252* A social and sports club (see GayBoxe below) with a comprehensive listing of gay, lesbian and transgender events and initiatives in Turin, throughout and outside Italy.

Fondazione Sandro Penna, via Santa Chiara 1, **T** 011 5212033. *1000-1700*. *Map 2, B3, p252* A library and research foundation for the historical study of and spread of knowledge about homosexuality.

Gay Boxe Italia, via Basilica 3/5, **T** 011 5211116. *1000-1700*. *Map 2, B5, p252* A gay sport and boxing club, part of the Circolo Maurice above.

Gay Lib Torino, **T** 0347 7629332 (mob.). Small, local based gay group for putting the gay community in touch with each other. The above number is a mobile which will be answered most of the time (within reason) or you can leave a message and be called back.

Informagay, via Giordano Bruno 80, **T** 011 3040934, www.informagay.it *1000-1700*. *Map 3, H7, p255* The Turin branch of the most wired national Italian gay/lesbian organisation. A good meeting place for the gay and lesbian community with loads of information on upcoming events, initiatives and demonstrations. Also a very comprehensive website.

Safonisba Anguissola, via Fabro 5, **T** 011 4342793 *1000-1700.*
Map 2, D3, p252 A gallery dedicated to exhibitions of lesbian
pictures, photography and sculpture.

ANLAIDS Regione Piemonte, via C Botta, **T** 011 4365541
1000-1700. Map 2, C1, p252 The Turin branch of the nationwide
Italian organisation offering scholarships and support for
anti-AIDS study and research.

Cafés and bars

Bridge Lesbo Bar, via Santa Maria Ausiliatrice 46/b,
T 011 4364952. *Map 2, A1, p252* Don't expect a quiet night
playing cards.

Caffe Leri, C.so Vittorio Emanuele II 64, **T** 011 543075. *Map 2, H5,
p252* Relaxed gay and lesbian café in the centre.

Dolci Alchimie, C.so Casale 2c, **T** 011 8192670. *Map 2, C12, p253*
Quiet café bar for both gays and lesbians.

Il Male Gay Pub, via Lombardore, **T** 011 284617. *Closed Tuesday.*
Map 1, C5, p250 Exactly what it says on the tin.

Le Vedove Allegre, via Don Bosco 69, **T** 011 482686. *Map 2, A4,
p252* A lesbian bar translating as 'the happy widows'.

Pasticceria Caffetteria Alfieri, via Borgomanero 49/c, **T** 011
746992. *Map 1, F3, p250* Fun café and patisserie for both gays
and lesbians.

Clubs

Alibi Club, via Mombarcaro 91, **T** 011 350433. *Map 1, I4, p251* Has a gay/lesbian night on Wednesday, Thursday and Saturday nights.

Metropolis Disco, via Principessa Clothidle 82, **T** 011 484116. *Map 1, C4, p250* Gay night on Thursday and Saturday.

Trailer, at the Centralino Club, via delle Rosine 16, **T** 0335 5349808. *Map 2, E10, p253* Has a gay night on Friday and Sunday nights.

Festivals

Every year in April the city hosts the **Turin Gay and Lesbian Film Festival**. For more information visit www.tglff.com

Hotels

Dal Conte B&B, via Conte Verde 1, **T** 011 4365300. *Map 2, C5, p252.* B&B with small rooms and an intimate setting.

Hotel Napoleon, via XX Settembre 5, **T** 011 5613223. *Map 2, G6, p252.* A three-star hotel for gays in the centre of town.

! The annual Gay and Lesbian film festival has brought directors like François Ozon, Gus Van Sant, Derek Jarman and Todd Haynes to an Italian audience. The 2004 festival celebrates the tenth anniversary of Jarman's death with a special homage to his work.

What the papers say...

"I carried the South American Handbook from Cape Horn to Cartagena and consulted it every night for two and a half months. I wouldn't do that for anything else except my hip flask."
Michael Palin, BBC Full Circle

"My favourite series is the Handbook series published by Footprint and I especially recommend the Mexico, Central and South America Handbooks."
Boston Globe

"If 'the essence of real travel' is what you have been secretly yearning for all these years, then Footprint are the guides for you."
Under 26 magazine

"Who should pack Footprint–readers who want to escape the crowd."
The Observer

"Footprint can be depended on for accurate travel information and for imparting a deep sense of respect for the lands and people they cover."
World News

"The guides for intelligent, independently-minded souls of any age or budget."
Indie Traveller

Mail order
Available worldwide in bookshops and on-line. Footprint travel guides can also be ordered directly from us in Bath, via our website www.footprintbooks.com or from the address on the credits page of this book.

Children in Italy are treated like members of Italy's long-lost royal family and so in hotels, shops, bars and restaurants you are unlikely to have any problems; quite the opposite in fact. Children are welcome at all hours and doted upon by waiters.

As a city, Turin is well-equipped to amuse children, although it is best to avoid walking down some of the seemingly endless boulevards – in fact the rickety old trams will probably provide ample fascination. It is unlikely that children will be interested in many of the churches and magnificent architecture (although some may love the stories and therefore locations of 'Black Magic Turin' – see p56); the following are a few recommendations that are bound to capture the little ones' attention.

The golden age of transport

A rickety 1930s train takes you up to the Basilica di Superga.

Sights

Funicular up to the Basilica di Superga , strada Basilica di Superga 73, **T** 011 8997456. *Map 1, A8, p250. See also p60.*
More about the journey than the destination, a ride in the 1930s cabin up to the Basilica is a ready-made fairground attraction.

★ **La Mole Antonelliana**, via Montebello 20. *Map 2, C9, p253. See also p49.* Take your little ones on a ride on the *ascensore panoramico* lift up this extraordinary monument to enjoy vertiginous views over the city.

Museo dell'Automobile, C.so d'Italia 40, **T** 011 677666. *Tues-Sun 1000-1830, Thurs until 2200, free. Map 1, J7, p251. See also p79.* It might be a bit of a boys' thing, but this collection of old and fast cars is bound to have would-be racing drivers dreaming.

Kids

★ **Museo Egizio**, via Accademia delle Scienze 6, **T** 011 561 7776. *Open every day except Mon 0830-1930. € 6.20 , € 3.10 for EU citizens aged 18-25. Guided tours every Sat. Free to holders of Torino Card. Map 2, D7, p253. See also p67.* Of all the museums this is perhaps the most appropriate for children. Not so much the smaller artifacts, but the mummies and spooky tombs will surely have them awestruck (if not a little scared!).

Museo della Marionetta, via Santa Teresa 5. *Map 2, E5, p252. See also p84.* If Punch and Judy goes down a treat, then so will this little museum to the Italian equivalent and with many other puppets from all over the world.

★ **Museo Nazionale del Cinema**, via Montebello 20, **T** 011 8125658. *Tues-Sun 0900-2000, Sat until 2300, Mon closed. € 5.20. Map 2, C9, p253. See also p50.* The cinema museum has lots of fun and interactive elements and curious galleries for them to enjoy.

★ **Il Parco Valentino**, C.so Massimo d'Azeglio. *Map 2, H11, p253. See also p73.* The best place for children to let off steam. From the botanical gardens to the facsimile medieval village and fort, there is lots for them to explore and enjoy here. Alternatively take them on a short river ride on the Po.

Sports

Skiing and other winter sports
What bigger playground could children want than the Alps, ski resorts and fresh air a little over an hour away in either the Val di Susa, see p110, or further north in the Val d'Aosta, see p113.

Turin is also well-served by **swimming pools**, see Sport, p204.

Airport information:

Aeroporto Sandro Pertini – Caselle T 011 5676361. **Flight information T** 011 5676361/2 (0600-2400). **Tourist information T** 011 5678124 (0830-2230). **Lost and found T** 011 5676200 (0800-2400). **Ticket office T** 011 5676373 (0530-2030). **Bank/exchange T** 011 5678198. **Business centre T** 011 5678345. **First aid T** 011 5676885. **Police/immigration T** 011 5679711.

Banks and ATMs

Banks are open from 0830-1330 and 1430-1530 on weekdays, closed on Saturdays and Sundays. Cash machines are available at most banks and most accept Visa, Eurocheque and other international cards. The city's main bank branches are along via Roma, via Cernaia, via Lagrange and via Roma.

Bicycle/moped hire

Amici della Bicicletta, via Vitt. Amedeo 21, **T** 011 5611481. **Bici e Dintorni**, via Andorno 35, **T** 011 888981. **Riscio**, viale Virgilio, **T** 011 605 1241, 1000-1900. **Velo**, via Sacchi 3 (in Porta Nuova station), **T** 011 6653661, 0430-0230. See also Sports, p199.

To hire a **vespa** or other **motorino** (moped):
Domina, **T** 011 744892. **Euroway**, C.so Sebastopoli 44/46, **T** 011 3195558. **Ruoto**, via Fontanesi and C.so Vittorio Emanuele II, no tel.

Car hire

All the major car rental companies have offices at the airport at the domestic arrivals point. In addition the following companies have offices in downtown: **Avis**, Porta Nuova station and via Nizza 2, **T** 011 4701528/5678020. **Europcar**, via Madam Cristin 72, **T** 011 6503603. **Hertz**, via Magellano 12, **T** 011 502080. **Sixt**, via Mongrando 48, **T** 011 836385.

Credit card lines
Amex T 06 72900347 or **T** 06 72282. **Diners T** 800 8864064 or
T 06 3213841. **Mastercard T** 800 870866 or **T** 800 872050. **Visa**
T 800 877232 or 002 348840001.

Dentists
Contact the main hospital (see below).

Disabled
Italy is a bit behind when it comes to catering for the disabled
but Turin is better than most Italian cities. Contact an agency
before departure for more details such as **Accessible Italy**,
www. accessibleitaly.com or **Vacanze Serene, T** 800271027.

Doctors
Two useful emergency numbers for doctors are:
T 011 5747 for adult patients, **T** 011 5621606 for children, or
contact main hospital (see below). EU citizens should take their
E111 with them.

Electricity
Italy functions on a 220V mains supply with a two-pin plug.

Embassies and consolates
Austria, C.so Matteotti 28, **T** 011 5635976. **Belgium**, via
Lamarmora Alfonso 39, **T** 011 5805101. **Denmark**, cia San
Secondo 33, **T** 011 5819274. **France**, via Roma 366, **T** 011
5619529. **Germany**, C.so Vittorio Emanuele II 98, **T** 011 531088.
Great Britain, via Saluzzo 60, **T** 011 6509202. **Netherlands**,
C.so Francia 131, **T** 011 7509612. **Norway**, via Giacosa Giuseppe
31, **T** 011 655385. **Spain**, piazza Castello 139, **T** 011 5627446.
Sweden, via dell'Arcivescovado 1, **T** 011 5172465. There is no
consular representation for the **USA** in Turin. Contact the embassy
or consulate in Rome or Milan respectively.

Emergency numbers

Police T 112. **Ambulance T** 118 or **T** 113. **Fire T** 115. **Red Cross T** 118. **Road relief/help T** 803116.

Hospitals

Molinette, C.so Bramante 88/90, **T** 011 6335294. **Mauriziano**, largo Turati 62, **T** 011 8151244. **Sant'Anna** (for children), C.so Spezia 60, **T** 011 3134420. **Maria Vittoria**, **T** 011 4393111.

Internet/email

Free access:

Informacitta, piazza Palazzo di Città 9/a, **T** 011 4422888 – 30 mins free access, no use of discs, printing or downloading. **Punto Informasette**, C.so Belgio 38, **T** 011 883251, 0900-1300, 1430-1620, Fri 0900-1300. **Infopoint dell'Universita di Torino**, via Po 29, T011 6703020, 0900-1900. **Biblioteca Civica Centrale**, via della Cittadella, T011 4429813, Mon-Fri 0830-1930, Sat 0900-1800. **Biblioteca Civica Torino Centro**, via della Cittadella 5, T011 4429826, Mon-Fri 0830-1930, Sat 0900-1800. **Biblioteca Nazionale**, piazza Carlo Alberto 3, T011 889737. **Centro Informagiovani**, via Galimberti 3, T011 6819433. **Info Point Europa**, via Lagrange 2, T011 5611988.

Paying access:

Thenetgate, via Carlo Alberto 1, **T** 011 8129844. **Soundtown**, via Berthollet 25, **T** 011 6696331. **Cremeria Alica**, piazza Statuto 9, **T** 011 5628890.

Left luggage

Both Porta Nuova and Porta Susa stations have left luggage offices.

Libraries

Biblioteca Civica Centrale, via della Cittadella, **T** 011 4429813, Mon-Fri 0830-1930, Sat 0900-1800. **Biblioteca Civica Torino**

Centro, via della Cittadella 5, **T** 011 4429826, Mon-Fri 0830-1930, Sat 0900-1800. **Biblioteca Nazionale**, piazza Carlo Alberto 3, **T** 011 889737.

Lost property

There are lost property (*oggetti smarriti*) offices at the airport and at Porta Nuova station. If you lose an ID report it to the police. Also: **Ufficio Oggetti Smarriti**, via Spoleto 9, **T** 011 4424293, Mon, Wed, Fri 0900-1200.

Media

English and other language **newspapers** are available from kiosks at the station and around the main squares of piazza Castello and piazza San Carlo.

Italian **television** has 7 terrestrial channels with occasional good programmes between the topless chat shows. The new pay TV platform, *Sky Italia* has a wide range of channels and continues to be Italy's only really outlet for anything approaching intellectual or artistic television. Turin's local newspaper is *La Stampa*, part of the Agnelli empire, and is acknowledged as an authoritative independent voice. Be a local and buy it at 0200 in the morning from one of the street vendors at traffic lights.

Pharmacies

Boniscontro, C.so Vittorio Emanuele II 66, **T** 011 541271, is a late-night pharmacy. For an emergency pharmacist call the **Farmaco Pronto** on **T** 800 218489.

Police

Carabinieri, via Valfre 5, **T** 011 55191/5629668; **Questura** (main police station), C.so Vinzaglio 10, **T** 011 55881. The police emergency telephone is **T** 112. You can also call the **Polizia Municipale**, **T** 011 4606060.

Post offices

Main post office: via Alfieri 10, **T** 011 803160 (reachable only from Italy), Mon-Fri 0830-1900, Sat 0830-1300.
The hours of business for smaller offices are 0830-1330, Mon-Sat. A first class stamp costs € 0.62, € 0.41 for a postcard. Postcards arrive quicker if you put them in an envelope. Call **T** 160 for information on other rates.
The central Italian postal information number is **T** 160.

Public holidays

1st Jan- New Year's Day; 6th Jan – Epiphany; 25th April – Liberation Day; 1st May – Labour Day; 24th June – San Giovanni – patron saint's day; 15th August – Assumption; 1st Nov – All Saints; 8th December – Immaculate Conception; 25th Dec – Christmas; 26th Dec – St Stephen's. See p183 for local festivals.

Religious services

Visit the following website for information on the timings of services in the city's churches: www.comune.torino.it/chiese

Student organisations

There are two main student organizations for Italians (ie they are not really needed by visitors), ARCI and AICS. The membership allows access to a number of Turin's clubs and bars (although you can do this if you simply produce ID and aren't seen going too often without subscribing) and also discounts in cinemas and sports clubs. Membership can be made on the door at any of the appropriate clubs (see Bars and clubs).

Taxi firms
Pronto Taxi T 011 5737; **Radio Taxi T** 011 5730; at **Porta Nuova station T** 011 547331; at **Porta Susa station T** 011 5622535. For taxis with facilities for the handicapped **T** 011 58116.

Telephone
The city's dialling code is 011 and must be dialled before all numbers, even within the city. The prefix for Italy is +39. For directory enquiries call **T** 12.

Time
Italy is one hour ahead of Greenwich Mean Time.

Toilets
There are public toilets at the railway station. Otherwise you can use the toilets in bars and cafés although it is polite to ask (you may need to get a specific key) and sometimes you must buy a drink or sandwich first. The standard of public and café-bar ablutions has improved greatly in recent years although there is still the odd hole in the ground souvenir here and there.

Transport enquiries
Bus enquiries T 011 3000611, www.sadem.it **Airport enquiries** Aeroporto Sandro Pertini – Caselle **T** 011 5676361; **Train enquiries** www.trenitalia.com

Travel agents
Citalia, Marco Polo House 3-5 Lansdowne Rd, Croydon **T** +44 208 686 5533, www.citalia.com/italy **Arblaster & Clarke Wine Tours**, **T**+44 1730 893344, www.arblasterandclark.com

Check out...

www...

100 travel guides, 100s of destinations, 5 continents
and 1 Footprint...

www.footprintbooks.com

A sprint through history

68,000 BC	First traces of civilization in the area with the Paleolithic Neanderthals
1800 BC	Pre-Indo-European Italic tribes such as the Ligures are resident in Piedmont
700 BC	Traces of Etruscan civilization in the Piedmont valleys and plain
218-202 BC	Hannibal crosses the Alps and encounters the Celtic-Ligurian Taurini tribe
191 BC	Turin and Piedmont become part of Cisalpine Gaul
23 BC	Turin falls under the rule of Emperor Augustus for 58 years
AD 58	The Roman colony of Colonia Giulia is founded on the site of modern Turin and renamed Augusta Taurinorum
AD 400-800	Turin comes under the rule of the Longobards, followed by the Franks
1200-1300	Turin becomes a medieval city state beset with internal rivalry and power struggles
1248	Control of Turin's Signoria with support of Emperor Frederick II. Save for brief periods, the Savoys will rule until 1861 and the reunification of Italy
1536	Turin is seized by Francois I of France. Turin is ruled from France until the Treaty of Chateau-Cambresis returns the city to the House of Savoy
1578	The Turin Shroud is brought from Chambery to Turin. Turin is made the capital of the Dukedom of Savoy by Emanuele Filiberto

1580- 1630	Reign of Carlo Emanuele I
1630- 37	Reign of Vittorio Amedeo I
1638-75	Reign of Carlo Emanuele II
1701	War of the Spanish Succession. Turin is allied with Austria and besieged by Franco-Spanish forces
1706	Battle of Turin. Franco-Spanish forces are repelled when Pietro Micca blows up underground tunnels underneath the citadel to prevent invasion
1713	Treaty of Utrecht. Vittorio Amedeo II is made King of Sicily until 1720
1720	Spanish take Vittorio Amedeo I's title and make him King of Sardinia instead
1797	Napoleon declares his Cisalpine Republic in Milan
1798	Under Napoleon, General Joubert's troops march into Turin and occupy the city. The Savoys are forced into exile
1802	Napoleon refers to the Italian part of the Cisalpine Republic as the 'Italian Republic'
1805	First mention, by Napoleon, of the concept of 'Italy'
1815	Napoleon is defeated at Waterloo and Turin is returned to the Savoy dukes
1848	Piedmont retains its independence from Austrian rule. Camillo Benso di Cavour publishes his 'Statuto' advocating a two-chamber parliament and an independent constitution for the Italian city states. Garibaldi returns from military exploits in South

America. Cavour and Garibaldi work together. Carlo Alberto grants a constiution based on Cavour's Statuto

1850	Cavour is made Prime Minister and forges an alliance with Napoleon III to defeat the Austrians
1857-71	The first tunnel through the Alps, the Frejus tunnel, is built and opened for trains
1859	Under Vittorio Emanuele II and with the help of Napoloeon III, the Austrians are defeated at the Battle of San Martino-Solferino. Milan and Lombardy are incorporated into the nascent Italian state
17 Mar 1861	The Kingdom of Italy is declared with Turin as its capital and Vittorio Emanuele II as its first King
1865	Florence is made the capital of Italy
1899	Fiat (Fabbrica Italiana Automobili di Torino) is founded
1906	Lancia is founded (also in Turin)
1910	Unrest at spiralling inflation. King Umberto I is assassinated
1913	Male suffrage is granted by Turin's Giovanni Giolitti
1900-14	The rise of Turin and Italy's trade unions
1915	A strike takes place in the Fiat factory, protesting against Italy's entry into the First World War
1920	A national workers' strike leads to the birth in Turin of Italy's Communist Party, the PCI, under Antonio Gramsci

1939-45	South and central Turin are badly hit by Allied bombs during the Second World War. Turin's war industry is a major target
1950-60	Turin experiences an industrial boom attracting mass immigration by southern Italians, especially to work on the Fiat factory floor
1965	The Mont Blanc tunnel is opened
1960-70	The output of cars by Fiat increases from 425,000 cars per year to 1.2 million
1969	Fiat buys the prestigious Ferrari sports car stable
1970	The Brigate Rosse left-wing terrorist group is born on the Fiat factory floor. 1973-80 become known as the *Anni di Piombo* (years of lead) with many terrorist attacks, notably on Milan and Bologna
1978	Fiat buys Lancia
1986	Fiat buys Milan-based Alfa Romeo
1980	The Frejus car tunnel is opened
1994	Serious floods in the region cause 68 deaths
1999	Turin awarded the Winter Olympics for 2006
2000	Fiat begins a long crisis and is forced to sell off its non-core assets
2003	Gianni Agnelli, l'Avvocato and Godfather of Fiat dies leaving the dynasty with doubts over succession. Agnelli's brother is considered the rightful and most appropriate heir

Art and architecture

500-400 BC The area at the confluence of the rivers Dora and Po is populated by a Ligurian tribe, the Taurini. Traces of their existence, the results of excavations, are on show at the Museo Civico d'Arte Antica

218 BC The Ligurian settlement is laid to waste by Hannibal en route to the Alps

28 BC Roman Turin Roman Emperor Augustus refounds the Roman settlement of Colonia Giulia (so-named during the reign of Julius Caesar) Augusta Taurinorum. The settlement is centred around the piazzale Cesare Augusto. The city has four gates at each point of the compass and 6-m high surrounding walls

AD 568-1248 After the fall of the Roman Empire, Turin falls under the Longobard kings until AD 773 and subsequently under the Franks until AD 888. Few or no traces remain of these reigns. Thereafter the city is torn between papacy and the rule of the commune, as Italy's city-states develop. In 1248 the Savoys arrive. After a period of conflict the torinese finally accept Savoy rule in 1274 AD. However, the first Savoys rule from nearby Pinerolo until 1418. Turin shows little evidence of Renaissance thinking and expression in its art and architecture. The cathedral of San Giovanni by Guarino Guarini is the only trace of Renaissance architecture extant in Turin today

1404 The University of Turin is founded. Plans are laid for many castles and palaces in and around Turin

16th century In 1536 Piedmont falls under French control. Emanuele Filiberto is installed as Savoy ruler and

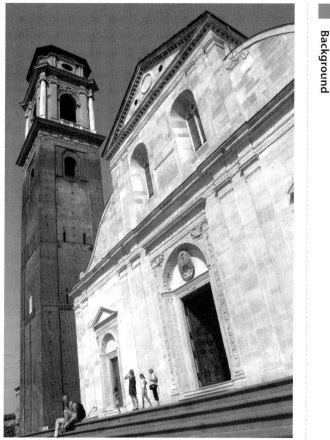

★ **A majestic backdrop**
*Turin's cathedral is the only remnant of Renaissance architecture in the city
with a striking classical white marble façade.*

chooses Turin as the capital of his duchy. Between 1564-66 the citadel on via Cernaia is built. Only the keep remains. During this period Turin undergoes radical change. Plans are laid for a 'zona di commando' group of official buildings around piazza Castello. The Turin Shroud is brought to Turin from Chambery

In 1584 Ascanio Vitozzi draws up a programme of rational town planning hailing the beginnings of Turin as a modern city of geometric grids. The foundations of modern day via Roma are laid, known then as the 'contrada nuova'. Emphasis is placed on the creation of squares and in displays of imperial power. The prospect of patronage, employment, wealth and fame attracts goldsmiths, thinkers, architects and painters from all over Italy

17th century

Vitozzi's plans are taken up by Carlo di Castellamonte and the years 1620 and the period 1630-37 see rapid urban development. Among the artists working on Turin's religious and public buildings at this time are Giacomo Rossignolo, Federico Zuccari, Cesare Arbasia and Antonio Parentani

Under the reign of Carlo Emanuele I many valuable works are acquired including works by Caravaggio. Works by representatives of the Bolognese school, Guido Reni, Domenichino and Guercino, are also imported. Carlo di Castellamonte opens up piazza San Carlo and in 1646-58 his son Amedeo designs the façade of the Palazzo Reale. Turin's distinctive baroque style is shaped by the Modenese architect, Guarino Guarini, whose oeuvre includes the church of San Lorenzo, the chapel of the Holy Shroud, the Accademia delle Scienze and Palazzo Carignano

18th century

The Savoys wish Turin to emulate, if not better, other European capitals. Following his death, Guarini is succeeded as royal architect by the Sicilian Filippo Juvarra. His work in Turin in the early part of the century hails the architecture of the Enlightenment that will become the fashion throughout Europe. Three of his most seminal works are the Basilica of the Superga (1715-31), the Palazzo Madama (1718-21) and the royal hunting lodge at Stupinigi (1729), as well as the famous Scala delle Forbici, scissor-staircase, in the Palazzo Reale. The latter part of the century sees the creation of the Borgo Po and Borgo Dora outside the city walls as the city expands

19th century

Neoclassicism and echoes of Haussman's Paris characterize this period with wide boulevards (Corso Vittorio Emanuele II and the via Roma), classical squares (piazza Vittorio Veneto) and bridges (Ponte Umberto) all designed to unify the city. The Unification of Italy in 1861 sees a boom in bold nationalistic architecture. The shift from baroque to neoclassical is masterminded by Juvarra's successor, Benedetto Alfieri. Buildings and creations include the parco Valentino and the church of the Gran Madre di Dio, as well as the Mole Antonelliana, which places Turin at the forefront of the international cities of art. The 1884 Expo sees the creation of the facsimile medieval village and citadel in the parco Valentino. Meanwhile, the Savoy Kings oversee the creation of the Galleria Sabauda and the expansion of the Egyptian collection creates the Museo Egizio

1900   The premiere of Tosca is held in the Reggio in Turin

1902   Turin hosts Italy's first international art expo, featuring the art nouveau style for the first time, leading to its Italian expression as lo stile Liberty

1904   The Italian film industry is born in Turin. In 1914 the seminal Italian film, *Cabiria* is shot in Turin's film studios. Although the industry's main studios will in due course move south to Rome, Turin retains its status as Italian cinema's spiritual home. Meanwhile, Turin's industrial base makes it the concrete expression of the ideas of Futurismo

1929-30   Mussolini commissions the Lingotto Fiat factory with its famous rooftop testing track. He also orders the renovation of via Roma with its marble arcades, a Utopian-Fascist version of the Roman style

1959   The Galleria d'Arte Moderna is opened. Pop Art, Dada and Arte Povera all flourish in Turin

1961   Celebrating 100 years of the unified Italian state, Palazzo del Lavoro and Palazzo Vela are built, designed by Pier Luigi and Rigotti Nervi respectively

1969   *The Italian Job* is filmed in Turin

1988 to the present day   The Lingotto complex is converted into an expo and conference centre by Renzo Piano. Turin puts into place a long-term plan to reconfigure its public transport structure. Coincidentally to this Turin is elected as host of the 2006 Winter Olympics

Books and films

Turin has not received the same reverence among writers as Florence, Venice or Rome, falling largely off the radar of the travellers of the 19th-century. The city generally receives a cursory mention in Italian narratives, focusing mainly on the city's location, architecture and political importance. The following all contain good introductions to Italy with scant reference to Turin.

Travel writing

Byron, *Letters*. Typically flowery musings, extravagant statements and clever-dick comments in epistles.

Dickens, C, *Pictures from Italy* (1998), Penguin. Travelogue of refreshingly unblinkered observations and descriptions.

Goethe, W, *Italian Journey* (1970), Penguin. Beautifully written descriptions mixed with more abstract musings from the original Romantic smitten by Italy.

James, Henry, *Italian Hours* (1995), Penguin Classics. Contains a surprising and generous description of Turin.

Moreton, H V, *A Traveller in Italy* (2001), Methuen. A gentlemanly and scholarly account infused with local detail and encounters with the natives.

St Aubain de Teran, L, *Elements of Italy* (2001), Virago. Excerpts of wistful and descriptive accounts of the best of Italy.

Stendhal, H, *Italian Journey*, Penguin. Romantic and flowery travelogue by the master 19th-century French novelist.

Contemporary non-fiction

Barzini, L, *The Italians* (1968), Penguin. At times almost a character/nation assassination, all the more incredible in that it is written by an Italian. Possibly the most incisive piece of writing there is on the Italian mindset and on the illusion that is Italy.

Richards, C, *The New Italians* (1995), Penguin. A refreshing account of Italy and the Italians at the end of the 20th century that dispels the myths of Chiantishire and Bella Tuscany.

Fiction and poetry

Primo Levi (*The Periodic Table* and *If This is a Man*) was born and lived in Turin on Corso Umberto until his suspicious death in 1987, as did **Carlo Levi** (*Cristo si e' fermato ad Eboli*), **Friedrich Nietszche**, when writing *Ecce Homo*, and **Natalia Ginzburg**. Turin features most of all however in the novels and poetry of **Cesare Pavese** (such as *La Luna e il Falo*) who was born and lived nearby.

The current best-selling novelist and commentator, **Alessandro Baricco**, published in the UK by Harvill Press, was also born in Turin. His most famous book, *Silk* (1997), is available in translation.

Calvino, I, *Numbers in the Dark* (1996), Vintage. A collection of short stories, some set in Turin and its "streets that never end".

Films

One film stands above all others in Turin – Peter Collinson's 1969 classic, *The Italian Job*, a superb caricature of Anglo-Italian relations starring Michael Caine, Noel Coward and Benny Hill and the immortal line, "You're only supposed to blow the bloody doors off!"

Turin is also the setting of many Italian horror classics, notably from Italy's Hitchcock, **Dario Argento**. *Deep Red* (*Profondo Rosso* – 1975) is perhaps the most famous, as well as more recently *I Can't Sleep* (*Non ho Sonno*), starring Max von Sydow.

Two other Italian neo-realist classics recounting the trials and tribulations of 1950s and 1960s Sicilian émigrés are *La Donna della Domenica* (1975) by **Luigi Comencini** and *Cosi Ridevano* (1998) by **Gianni Amelio Rosso**.

Turin and the Italian Job

Turin deserves a special place in the hearts of British cinema-goers. It was here that in 1969 Charlie Croker, the swaggering cockney played by Michael Caine, was sent by Noel Coward (in his last screen performance) along with Benny Hill and a bunch of public school rally drivers to steal four million dollars in gold from under the noses of the Italian government "to help with Britain's balance of payments." Dusted off for its 30th anniversary in 1999, the film, a masterpiece of pastiche and chauvinism, has undergone something of a retro renaissance: the line about "blowing the bloody doors off" was recently voted the best-loved cinema line of all time and the film inspired a recent remake/sequel. But it is a testament to the general ignorance of Turin's treasures and assets that the American remakers decided to set their film in Venice. How, you might ask, would it be possible to have cinema's most famous car-chase in Venice, a city whose streets are so famously full of water?

Turin occupies a scenic location in the foothills of the Italian Alps, under the teeth of Mont Blanc and the Matterhorn. The film opens with Beckermann sweeping through breathtaking Alpine scenery in his Lamborghini Miura to the accompaniment of Matt Monroe's Quincey Jones-arranged version of 'On Days like These' – only to meet his end in the jaws of a JCB hidden in a tunnel by the mafia.

Unlike the concentric chaos of most Italian towns, Turin's historic centre is laid out in a symmetrical grid of regal and imperial boulevards. When the convoy escorting the gold bullion arrives it turns left by the grandiose Porta Nuova station and up the via Roma, the city's central column, through the baroque piazza San Carlo. There's a traffic jam, but this is the home of Juventus and there's a football match, so it's normal! The convoy advances slowly up this majestic avenue, redesigned by Mussolini with grand utopian marble columns, and bordered with arcades of baroque arches and capitals. Now, as then, these shaded arches are home to the city's most luxuriant and decadent bars and cafés, and its most boastful and expensive clothes shops.

Turin's Parisian symmetry turns out to be its downfall as Caine, disguised as a football fan, is able to make his way through a network of courtyards and inter-connecting arches to the via Accademia delle Scienze, which runs parallel with via Roma, and seemingly drive straight into the ornate marble foyer of the Museo Egizio. Here, he establishes his lair but this scene in fact took place in the Palazzo Madama with its wonderful interior staircase. It is here that Croker delivers his pep talk reminding the gang that "in this country they drive on the wrong side of the road..."

At the delta of via Roma is piazza Castello – a grand, typically cobbled square, seething with confused rivers of hooting cars and trams. This is the centre of the traffic jam masterminded by Benny Hill's dirty-old-man. When the traffic lights start going mad, it is here that the choirboys start gambling and smoking, the old man falls asleep with his foot on his horn, and the Latin lover gets his face slapped for stroking the face of a woman stuck in the traffic going the other way.

Marco Buttolo, who was then a director of Turin's Vigili Urbani traffic control brigade, was involved in the co-ordination of the traffic jam. He remembers fondly his collaboration with the film's producers: "It wasn't very hard" he adds, "traffic jams like that happened regularly, it was just a matter of keeping it jammed and not telling anyone why while we filmed". Rumour has it that L'Avvocato, Gianni Agnelli, was also very supportive of the film and as patriarch of the city was able to make anything happen as the director wished.

Nowadays, piazza Castello is a much calmer place. A fountain provides for much calmer contemplation of the square's splendours: the centrepiece Palazzo Madama, the ornate balconies and window-trimmings of the burgeoning and recently modernized opera house; a McDonalds; and most importantly the faded grandeur of the Palazzo Reale, reminiscent of Versailles and once the seat of the Italian Royal Family. The piazza is almost entirely given over to these, and the former chaos a mere echo.

Back on via Roma, when the convoy draws level, the gang pounces and tows the unsuspecting bullion van into the museum. Having transferred the gold, the red, white and blue Minis then set off all over Turin in one of British cinema's most famous car chases.

First they roar and bump sacrilegiously down the museum's baroque staircases, through the arched entrance and back out on to via Roma, seemingly back into danger. Here, on the pavements they weave in and out of the arcades, eluding blundering *carabinieri* on motorcycles, grabbing a bite to eat and disrupting the leisurely *passeggiatas* of the locals. Photogenic and cinematically irresistible, the sequence is actually composed of many shots of the Minis going up and down different sections of the same arcades in via Roma and piazza San Carlo.

From here they descend into the city's lone pedestrian subway giving the director the excuse to emerge in suburban Turin outside the Palazzo a Vela. It is here that the Minis lead a lone *carabiniere* up the ramp only for his Alfa Romeo to break down. Apparently permission to film on top of the Palazzo a Vela came about through a linguistic misunderstanding. The producers asked for permission to put a 'macchina' up on the roof, but 'macchina', unless specified, means both camera and car!

After this the film jumps to an unconnected set piece on the rooftop testing track of the Lingotto complex, the former Fiat factory. Here, after leading the police a merry little waltz, the Union

Jack coloured Minis head back into town, jumping a famous 70-ft gap between the buildings of the Fiat factory, and skirting the edge of the romantic parco Valentino, and arriving at the rivers edge.

Here (but actually on the other bank), a wedding party is filing out of the neoclassical church of the Gran Madre, only to be unceremoniously disturbed by the cars zooming out and criss-crossing down over the steps in front of them. In reality this is impossible since the area behind the church is basically a dead end. From here, opposite Piazza Vittorio, they dive into the Po, and cross the weir to the riverside Murazzi. Here, on the platforms of former cargo bays, Turin's sun-drenched youth are out enjoying a relaxing cappuccino when suddenly they find their chairs and tables swept into the river. This area is given over today to cafés and bars to the clubs of Turin's vibrant alternative music scene.

The final urban scene is the famous chase through the drain that leads out again into the Alpine countryside. This drain does not exist in Turin. It was in fact the Birmingham-Coventry Tithebarn Main Sewer, which was under construction at the time.

Whilst not the most curious of tourists, Michael Caine and his 'Self-Congratulation Society' could be forgiven for not stopping to take in the understated treasures of this underrated city. They were only interested in its gold. "Within two hours we'll be across the Alps and into Switzerland". Only a few minutes later not only the fortunes of the British treasury but the fate of the whole ill-starred gang hangs very much in the balance... in a bus off the edge of a cliff.

Every year in November, UK-based group *The Italian Job Rally* runs a homage-cum-booze cruise to Italy and back. You don't have to have a Mini or an Aston but other cars are frowned upon. They can be contacted at 93 Hangleton Road, Hove, East Sussex, BN3, **T** 01273 418100, www.geocities.com/motorcity/2706/ijrally.htm

Facts and information about the film and sequel are found on the following websites: www.italianjobmovie.com and www.codesign.it/codework/italian

Language

Local dialect

'Normal' Italian is generally spoken in Turin, but the Piemontese dialect is still very evident and proudly retained, particularly among the older generations although you will find that most of the young also know a good deal of phrases. You will hear this dialect particularly in the markets and backwaters of the city, and even more so out in the country where there are even sub-dialects. The dialect of the Val d'Aosta is even stronger. Here French is given equal status while the patois itself is an alpine mish-mash of French, Italian and Swiss-German. So don't be surprised if you don't always understand what's being said – it's nothing to do with your school Italian. There are even some Italians, especially those who have immigrated from the south, who are at a loss. The Piemontese accent has a pronounced, rather ugly elongated 'e', as in 'piemont –ee-se' and also by the tendency to pronounce vowels in a French way, 'eu' instead of 'u' and to clip the end of words, rather like Catalan Spanish. A few phrases or local twists you might here are 'andumma' instead of 'andiamo' (let's go), 'as vedumma' instead of 'ci vediamo' (see you later) and 'te sbreuta' instead of 'sbrigati' (hurry up). 'Cin cin' is the local equivalent of 'salute' (cheers – before drinking) now used throughout northern Italy.

Gestures

Italians are famously theatrical and animated in dialogue and often resort to a variety of gestures to accompany, or in some cases substitute, words. Knowing a few of these will help you understand what's being implied to you:

Side of left palm on side of right wrist as right wrist is flicked up – go away

Hunched shoulders and arms lifted with palms of hands outwards – what am I supposed to do?!

Thumb, index and middle finger of hand together, wrist upturned and shaking – what the hell are you doing/what's going on?!

Both palms together and moved up and down in front of stomach – ditto (Note: both these gestures are actually supposed to be simulating male masturbation but are commonly used by all ages and genders)

All fingers of hand squeezed together – to signify a place is packed full of people

Front or side of hand to chin – to signify 'nothing', as in 'I don't understand' or 'I've had enough'

Flicking back of right ear – to signify someone is gay

Index finger in cheek – to signify nice food

Basics

Good morning *Buongiorno/Salve*
Good evening *Buona sera*
Good night *Buona notte*
Goodbye *Arrivederci*
Please *Per favore*
Thankyou *Grazie*
Not at all, a pleasure *Prego*
Hello, goodbye *Ciao*
Hello? (when answering the phone) *Pronto*
Yes *si*
No *no*

Questions

Excuse me *Mi scusi* (formal)/*Scusami* (informal)
Where is the station? *Dove si trova la stazione*

What's your name? *Come ti chiami?*
My name is... *Io mi chiamo…*
Where do you live? *Dove abiti?*
Where are you from? *Di dove sei?*
I am English *(Io) sono inglese*
Do you speak English? *Parli inglese?*
What time is it? *Che ore sono?*
What time does the restaurant open/close? *A che ora apre/chuide il ristorante?*
It's 4 o'clock *Sono le quattro*

Numbers

One *Uno* Two *Due* Three *Tre* Four *Quattro* Five *Cinque* Six *Sei*
Seven *Sett* Eight *Otto* Nine *Nove* Ten *Dieci* Eleven *Undici*
Twelve *Dodici* Thirteen *Tredici* Fourteen *Quattordici*
Fifteen *Quindici* Sixteen *Seidici* Seventeen *Dicesette*
Eighteen *Diciotto* Nineteen *Dicenove* Twenty *Venti* Thirty *Trenta*
Forty *Quaranta* Fifty *Cinquanta* Sixty *Sessanta* Seventy *Settanta*
Eighty *Ottanta* Ninety *Novanta* One hundred *Cento*
One thousand *Mille*

Days of the week

Monday *Lunedi* Tuesday *Martedi* Wednesday *Mercoledi*
Thursday *Giovedi* Friday *Venerdi* Saturday *Sabato*
Sunday *Domenica*

Getting around

One ticket for... *un biglietto per...*
single *solo andata*
return andata e ritorno
airport *aeroporto*

bus stop *fermata*
train *treno*
car *macchina*
taxi *tassi*

Accommodation

a double/single room *una camera doppia/singola*
a double bed *un letto matrimoniale*
bathroom *bagna*
Is there a view? *c'é una bella vista?*
Can I see the room? *posso vedere la camera?*
When is breakfast? *a che ora è la colazione?*
Can I have the key? *posso avere la chiave?*

Shopping

this one/that one *questo/quello*
less *meno*
more *di più*
How much is it/are they? *quanto costa/costano?*
Can I have...? *posso avere...?*

Eating out

I'd like a beer please *Vorrei una birra per favore*
I'd like a glass of red/white wine please *Vorrei un bicchiere di vino rosso/bianco per favore*
I would like to make a reservation please *Vorrei fare una prenotazione per favore*
Is there a menu? *c'è un menù?*
Where's the toilet? *dov'è il bagno?*
The bill please *Il conto/la nota per favore*

Index

Credits

Footprint credits

Text editor: Laura Dixon
Map editor: Sarah Sorensen

Publisher: Patrick Dawson
Series created by Rachel Fielding
Cartography: Claire Benison, Kevin
Feeney, Robert Lunn
Proofreading: Stephanie Lambe
Design: Mytton Williams

Photography credits

Front cover: Corbis (old factory,
Ragazzini, Turin)
Inside: Julius Honnor
(p1 Urn, p5 Fiat, p31 La Mole
Antonelliana, p105 Stag, Stupinigi)
Back cover: Julius Honnor

Print

Manufactured in Italy by LegoPrint
Pulp from sustainable forests

Footprint feedback

We try as hard as we can to make
each Footprint guide as up to date as
possible but, of course, things always
change. If you want to let us know
about your experiences – good, bad
or ugly – then don't delay, go to
www.footprintbooks.com and send
in your comments

Publishing information

Footprint Turin
1st edition
Text and maps © Footprint
Handbooks Ltd November 2003

ISBN 1 903471 84 2
CIP DATA: a catalogue record for this
book is available from the British Library

Published by Footprint
6 Riverside Court
Lower Bristol Road
Bath, BA2 3DZ, UK
T +44 (0)1225 469141
F +44 (0)1225 469461
discover@footprintbooks.com
www.footprintbooks.com

Distributed in the USA by
Publishers Group West

Publishing stuff

Complete title list

For a different view…
choose a Footprint

More than 100 Footprint travel guides
Covering more than 150 of the world's most exciting
countries and cities in Latin America, the Caribbean, Africa,
Indian sub-continent, Australasia, North America, Southeast Asia,
the Middle East and Europe.

Discover so much more…
The finest writers. In-depth knowledge. Entertaining and
accessible. Critical restaurant and hotels reviews. Lively
descriptions of all the attractions. Get away from the crowds.

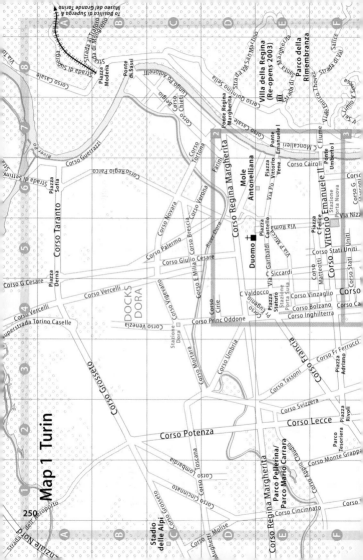

Map 1 Turin

250

To Basilica di Superga &
Museo del Grande Torino

Strada al Suo ...erga
Strada di Mongreno

Piazza
Modena

Ponte
di Sassi

Lungo Po Antonelli

Corso Casale

Corso Casale

Via ... della Maddalena

Villa della Regina
(Re-opens 2003)

Corso Quinto Sella

Parco della
Rimembranza

Ponte Regina
Margherita

Ponte Regina Margherita

Corso Casale

Ponte
Vittorio
Emanuele I

Fiume

Corso Guerrazzi

Corso Regio Parco

Corso Tortona

Corso Belgio

Corso Chieti

Farini

Piazza
Sofia

Piazza
Derna

Corso Taranto

Corso G Cesare

Corso Vercelli

Corso Vercelli

Superstrada Torino Caselle

Corso Novara

Corso Palermo

Corso Giulio Cesare

Corso E Milia

Corso Brescia

Corso Verona

Corso Regina Margherita

Mole
Antonelliana

Piazza
Vittoria
Vene

Via Po

Corso Cairoli

Ponte
Umberto I

Corso

Corso G

Via Roma

Duomo

Piazza
Castello

Via Garibaldi

Via Milano

Via Pietro Micca

Corso Vittorio Emanuele II

Piazza
C Felice

Stazione
Porta Nuova

Via Nizza

Corso Stati Uniti

Corso Matteotti

Corso Stati Uniti

Via Siccardi

Corso Vinzaglio

Corso Bolzano

Corso Inghilterra

Corso

Piazza
Statuto

Piazza
P Eugenio

Stazione
Porta Susa

Corso
Citie

Corso
V Valdocco

Corso Princ Oddone

Corso Principe Oddone

Stazione
Dora

Corso Giovevanu

Corso Mortara

Corso Venezia

DOCKS
DORA

Corso Umbria

Corso Grosseto

Corso Francia

Corso Fr Ferrucci

Corso Tassoni

Corso Adriano

Corso Svizzera

Corso Lecce

Piazza
Rivoli

Corso Potenza

Parco
Tesoriera

Corso Appio
Claudio

Corso Monte Grappa

Parco Pellerina/
Parco Mario Carrara

Corso Regina Margherita

Corso
Cincinnato

Corso
Lombardia

Corso
Toscana

Stadio
delle Alpi

Corso Umbetti Molise

Corso Cincinnato

Corso

Via Ta

River Po

Strada di Settimo Sud

Viale della Thovez

V Sel...

V Umi...

Saffre

Strada di Val...

Strada di Fante ... Meghera

Ponte
Vittorio
Emanuele I

Monte ...

C Fiume

...nziale Nord dell'Aeroporto

Strada Nord

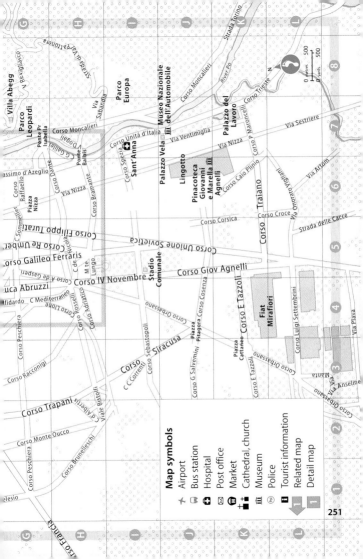

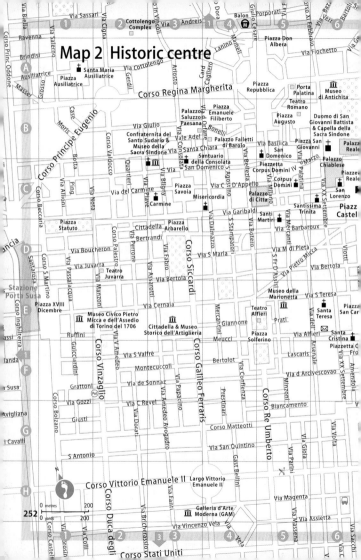

Map 2 Historic centre

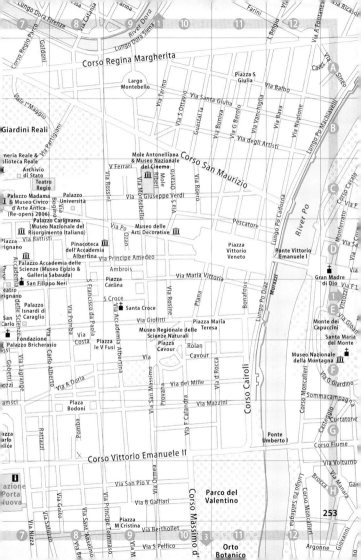

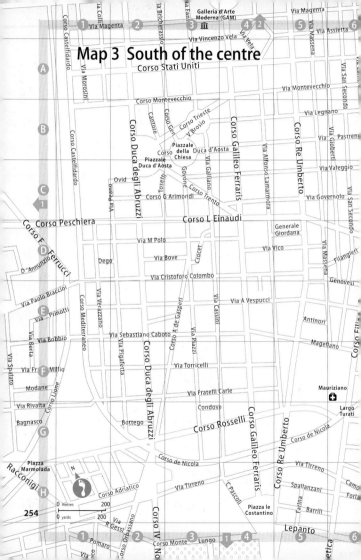

Map 3 South of the centre

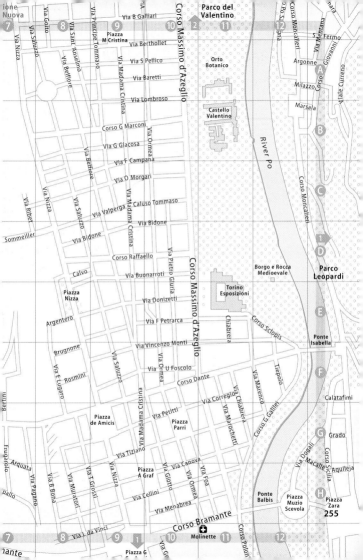

Parco del Valentino

Via B Galliari

Corso Massimo d'Azeglio

Piazza M Cristina

Via Berthollet

Via Principe Tommaso

Via Sant' Anselmo

Via Goito

Via Saluzzo

Via Nizza

Via S Pellico

Via Madama Cristina

Via Baretti

Via Belfiore

Via Lombroso

Orto Botanico

Corso Moncalieri

Corso Po Sagna

Corso Monfalieri

S Fermo

Via Mentana

Viale Curreno

Via Giovanni

Corso

Argonne

Milazzo

Marsala

A

B

Castello Valentino

Corso G Marconi

Via G Glacosa

Via Ormea

Via F Campana

Via O Morgari

Via Belfiore

Via Nizza

Via Ribet

Via Saluzzo

Via Valperga Caluso Tommaso

Via Madama Cristina

Via Bidone

Sommeiller

Via Bidone

Corso Raffaello

Calvo

Piazza Nizza

Via Buonarroti

Via Pietro Giuria

River Po

Corso Moncalieri

C

Corso Massimo d'Azeglio

Via Donizetti

Borgo e Rocca Medioevale

Torino Esposizioni

Parco Leopardi

D

E

Argentero

Brugnone

Via E Lugaro

Via Saluzzo

Via F Petrarca

Via Ormea

Via Vincenzo Monti

Chiabrera

Corso Sclopis

Ponte Isabella

F

Via Rosmini

Via U Foscolo

Corso Dante

Via Correglio

Via Chiabrera

Via Marchetti

Via Marenco

Corso G Galilei

Tiepolo

Calatafimi

Piazza de Amicis

Via Tiziano

Via T Grossi

Via Nizza

Via Madama Cristina

Via Petitti

Piazza Parri

G

Grado

Via Dogali

Corso Sicilia

Via Macallé

Aquileja

Arquata

Via Pagano

Via B Bona

Via Muratori

Via Saluzzo

Via Canova

Via Giotto

Via Ormea

Via Foa

Piazza A Graf

Via Cellini

Via Menabrea

Ponte Balbis

Piazza Muzio Scevola

Piazza Zara

H

255

Corso Bramante

Via L da Vinci

Molinette

Corso Poljon

Piazza G

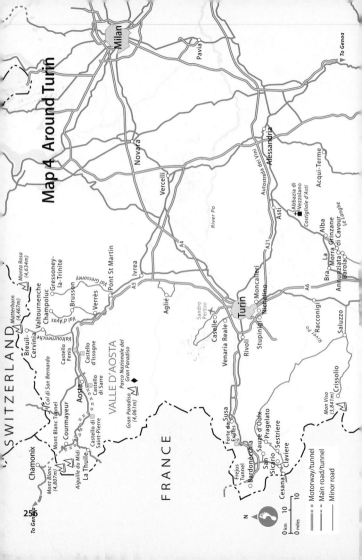

Map 4 Around Turin

SWITZERLAND

FRANCE

To Genoa

Milan

Pavia

Novara

Vercelli

Alessandria

Acqui-Terme

Abbazia di Vezzolano

Asti

Costigliole d'Asti

Alba

La Morra

Grinzane di Cavour

Barolo

Le Langhe

Annunziata

Bra

Autostrada dei Vini

A21

River Po

A4

Ivrea

A5

Pont St Martin

Val Gressoney

Monta Rosa (4,634m)

Matterhorn (4,467m)

Gressoney-la-Trinité

Champoluc

Brusson

Verrès

Valtournenche

Breuil-Cervinia

Val d'Ayas

Castello d'Issogne

Castello Fénis

Col di San Bernardo

Aosta

Castello di Sarre

Castello di Saint-Pierre

VALLE D'AOSTA

Parco Nazionale del Gran Paradiso

Gran Paradiso (4,061m)

Mont Blanc Tunnel

Courmayeur

La Thuile

Aiguille du Midi

Mont Blanc (4,807m)

Chamonix

To Genoa

Aglié

Sandro Pertini

Casello

Venaria Reale

Rivoli

Stupinigi

Turin

Moncalieri

Nichelino

A6

Racconigi

Saluzzo

Crissolo

Mon Viso (3,841m)

River Po

Forte di Susa

Exilles

San Sicario

Sauze d'Oulx

Pragelato

Sestriere

Cesana Claviere

Bardonecchia

Fréjus Tunnel

N

0 km   10

0 miles   10

Motorway/tunnel

Main road/tunnel

Minor road

256